The Future of Conservatism

RELIGION AND CONTEMPORARY CULTURE SERIES

Edited by Peter Augustine Lawler

Stuck with Virtue:
The American Individual and Our Biotechnological Future
Peter Augustine Lawler

Till We Have Built Jerusalem:
Architecture, Urbanism, and the Sacred
Philip Bess

The Future of Conservatism

Conflict and Consensus in the Post-Reagan Era

Edited by
Charles W. Dunn

ISI Books
Wilmington, Delaware
2007

The future of conservatism : conflict and consensus in the post-
Reagan era / edited by Charles W. Dunn.—1st ed.—Wilmington,
Del. : ISI Books, 2007.

p. ; cm.
(Religion and contemporary culture)

ISBN-13: 978-1-933859-22-4 (pbk.)
ISBN-10: 1-933859-22-9 (pbk.)
Includes index.

1. Conservatism—United States. 2. Conservatism—Religious
aspects. 3. Reagan, Ronald—Influence. 4. United States—Politics
and government—1989– 5. Religion and politics—United States.
I. Dunn, Charles W.

JC573 .F88 2007   2006936004
320.520973—dc22   0705

Book design by Jennifer M. Connolly

ISI Books
Intercollegiate Studies Institute
3901 Centerville Road
Wilmington, Delaware 19807
www.isibooks.org

Contents

Introduction

Conservatism on Center Stage

Charles W. Dunn

The future, as always, is veiled from our vision. But for the moment the conservative intellectual movement in America, born in the wilderness a generation ago, has undeniably achieved an unprecedented level of influence and importance.

George H. Nash[1]

CONSERVATISM, ONCE ON THE wings of the American political stage, now plays a leading role. But despite its emergence as a powerful political force, misunderstandings abound about conservatism's meaning and nature—economically, philosophically, politically, religiously, and socially.[2]

In 1860, Abraham Lincoln provided a succinct definition of conservatism at New York City's Cooper Union: "Is it not adherence to the old and tried, against the new and untried?"[3] But this simple understanding of conservatism masks important differences among its adherents. Indeed, American conservatism is best characterized by complexity, not simplicity. First, although it is commonly considered an ideology, many of conservatism's foremost intellectuals dispute this notion. Second, although it is often simply presented as a counterbalance to liberalism, conservatism's relationship to liberalism is complicated and contested. Third, although it is thought to embody a common set of principles, its principles frequently conflict. Fourth, although many leading intellectuals, liberal and conservative, believe that conservatism lacks a significant tradition in America, it has contributed more to American life than is usually acknowledged. Fifth, although it is usually thought to instill homogeneity among its adherents, in truth conservatism is marked by a great deal of intellectual heterogeneity. And sixth, although the public views it primarily as a political movement, conservatism's strength rests less in the realm of pragmatic politics than it does in the realm of ideas. In other words, conservatism in America is far from monolithic.

Conservatism Defined

Yet despite this complexity and the manifold differences among conservatives, the following definition captures the mainstream of conservative thought. Conservatism is the defense of inherited political, economic, religious, and social traditions from the forces of abrupt change, based upon the belief that to maintain continuity and stability in society, established customs, laws, and mores should guide change.

To amplify this definition by contrasting it with liberalism, conservatives generally (1) place more emphasis on orthodox and traditional religious values, (2) express less faith in the goodness, reason, and perfectibility of mankind, (3) voice greater opposition to the power of centralized government, (4) place a greater emphasis on state and local governments than they do the national government in the federal system, (5) identify with nationalism more than with internationalism, and as such tend to be less supportive of the United Nations and other international organizations, (6) express a more fervent patriotic spirit, (7) put greater emphasis upon the responsibilities and duties of individuals than upon their rights, (8) trust capitalism and free markets more than government regulation in determining economic policy, and (9) believe that gradual changes within existing institutions offer the best way to ensure society's economic, political, religious, and social health.

Ten Canons of Conservatism

This process of comparing conservatism to liberalism helps to give us an idea of its shape. But given the complexity of conservatism, does it offer a generally accepted set of principles? Do certain ideas almost always mark conservatism, regardless of its myriad manifestations? In a nutshell, can conservatism be boiled down to several readily identifiable canons? By synthesizing the conservative tenets articulated by a variety of conservative thinkers, it is possible to answer "yes" to this question. The ten canons presented here represent a sort of conservative intellectual synthesis.

First, continuity stands out as the most widely accepted canon of conservative thought, which comes as no surprise, because conservatives place a high value on order in society. Preferring organic change to revolution, conservatives oppose large-scale and abrupt alterations that disrupt and unsettle society. Their respect for the past reflects a desire to incorporate change within existing community institutions, standards, and traditions, making continuity from generation to generation the most essential canon of conservative thought.

Second, authority manifests itself as a natural corollary of conservatives' preference for continuity in social order. Conservatives believe that the government must protect society from foreign challenges and domestic disturbances that would disrupt the continuity of community, but critics sometimes attack conservatives for an apparent contradiction between supporting increased government spending for the protection of society and accusing the government of over-taxing and over-spending. But a coherent philosophy rests beneath this seeming contradiction. Because of a passion for order, conservatives believe that the government's primary function is to protect society against foreign threats and to keep order at home. Conservatives see the government as the most effective means of protecting against the selfish appetites of men, such aggression being manifest in both the aggression of foreign nations and domestic disregard for civil authority. On the other hand, because conservatives believe in incremental and organic change, they distrust efforts to alter society through centralized governmental power and planning—which, of course, require high taxes and spending. For conservatives, the primary purpose of government is to protect, not alter, organically developed human society.

Third, community must come near the top of a list of fundamental conservative tenets, for conservatives believe communities provide the structure for organic change and serve as a countervailing force against the power that is concentrated in government. Conservatives also believe that human flourishing is nourished by the individual's inclusion within a dense web of private and voluntary organizations, including professional associations, churches, service groups, universities, trade unions, newspapers, private businesses, and local governmental institutions.

Fourth, deity holds a place on most lists of conservative tenets, if for no other reason than this: conservatives usually believe in traditional moral values, and are distrustful of human nature. Put another way, they believe that natural or divine law transcends human law, which makes man and government ultimately accountable to God.

Fifth, duty or personal responsibility ranks higher in conservative thinking than does the concept of individual rights. When rights come to trump individual responsibilities, conservatives contend, citizens come to think more about what government can do for them rather than what they can, and ought to do for themselves. This leads not only to statism, but also to social and moral decay.

Sixth, democracy in the conservative mind exists within the context of a constitutional order carefully designed not only to limit and separate governmental power, but also to refine democratic opinion and encourage deliberation. Because the Constitution circumscribes in precise terms governmental activity, conservatives advocate its "strict interpretation," contending that the courts should interpret the law rather than make it, thereby observing the "original intentions" of the founders in framing the American constitutional system.

Seventh, property and its ownership enable individuals to have a greater stake in society, according to conservatives, who maintain that when people are tied in this concrete way to their communities, they are more likely to function as responsible citizens who desire to preserve the social order. A sound social order not only creates opportunities for people to own property, thereby strengthening their ties to the community, but it also helps them to rise in economic and social status. The opportunity to own property is therefore basic to a humane and free society.

Eighth, although conservatives value both liberty and equality, they consider liberty significantly more important to the vitality of society. A dynamic and developing society requires liberty to encourage creativity, and equality of opportunity to prevent serious social unrest. Conservatives believe that people have the right to equality of opportunity, but not equality of results. Arbitrary standards of equality, enforced by a burdensome and costly governmental bureaucracy, stultify and numb the desire of the individual to create and excel and, therefore, diminish the dynamic development of society. Totalitarianism, as in the former Soviet Union, emphasizes equality of results rather than equality of opportunity. And in some democracies, such as the Scandinavian countries, cradle-to-grave social welfare policies have driven tax rates to as high as 50 percent, crushing individual initiative and creativity.

Ninth, the principle of meritocracy reflects conservatives' belief that merit, or talent, ought to be the primary factor in the selection of leaders. Conservatives believe that orders and classes of people naturally exist in society and that the leadership class helps to provide order by guiding and governing society. Because the American founders rejected the idea of an aristocratic leadership class composed of titled nobles, conservatives in America believe in a "natural aristocracy" open to those whose ability qualifies them for membership.

Tenth, antipathy to communism abroad and a more intrusive central government at home, reflected in such legislative initiatives as the New Deal, Fair Deal, and Great Society, historically played a major role in bringing together conservatives of different persuasions during its formative years. Nearly all of the foremost conservative works of the 1940s and 1950s attacked the centralized state, a tendency taken to its extreme in communist nations.

The Emergence of Contemporary Conservatism

More than any other public figure in American history, Ronald Reagan manifested all of these tenets in his personal life and philosophy. Decisively influenced by the conservative intellectual movement of the post–World War II decades, he became America's most effective popularizer of the diverse strands of conservative political philosophy that emerged in the postwar era, which included both American and European thinkers.

In 1950 Lionel Trilling declared in *The Liberal Imagination* that in America "liberalism is not only the dominant but even the sole intellectual tradition. For it is the plain fact that nowadays there are no conservative . . . ideas in general circulation."[4] But even as Trilling chiseled an epitaph on the conservative tombstone, contemporary conservatism had already risen from the dead as a reaction to communism's rise internationally and to the emergence of a powerful central government in Washington after the Roosevelt and Truman administrations. These rapid changes, which struck at core conservative beliefs, sparked a remarkably effective intellectual backlash, both in America and abroad, that would culminate in Reagan's presidency.

In 1944 Friedrich von Hayek's *Road to Serfdom* challenged the rise of a state-managed economy, whether in the form of communism or New Deal liberalism.[5] In 1948 Richard Weaver's *Ideas Have Consequences* argued that the dominant ideas of liberalism would produce disastrous consequences for personal freedom and the social order.[6] In 1949 Ludwig von Mises' *Human Action* presented a powerful case for the superiority of free-market economics.[7] And also in 1949, Peter Viereck's *Conservatism Revisited* drew praise from *The Times of London* for laying out a set of traditional conservative principles based upon the ideas of British parliamentarian Edmund Burke.[8] These books represent but a few of the thoughtful presentations of conservatism that boldly attempted to resist liberalism's ascendancy in America's universities and public institutions.

Shortly thereafter, in rapid-fire succession between 1950 and 1953, there appeared on the scene many influential conservative books building upon the pioneering work of Hayek and Weaver, including but certainly not limited to William F. Buckley's *God and Man at Yale* (1951),[9] Eric Vogelin's *The New Science of Politics* (1952),[10] Russell Kirk's *The Conservative Mind* (1953),[11] Leo Strauss's *Natural Right and History* (1953),[12] and Robert Nisbet's *The Quest for Community* (1953).[13] All of these books, whether written before or after 1950, continue to enjoy significant influence more than five decades later among various schools of conservative thought.

Appearing like a double fortissimo on a musical score expressing the crescendo of influential conservative books, Clinton Rossiter's *Conservatism in America: The Thankless Persuasion* received the Charles A. Beard Memorial Prize in 1955. Rossiter's book not only won a major literary award, but it sparked a heated debate about the meaning of conservatism. Some viewed Rossiter's book as a defense of the mainstream or moderate center of American politics rather than as an effective counterweight to liberalism's hegemony. Regardless, conservatism had come of age.[14]

Not only have these writers had continuing influence for more than fifty years, but others have followed in their footsteps, including Pulitzer and Nobel Prize winners. Among the leading conservative authors and their books since the mid-1950s are Milton Friedman, *Capitalism and Freedom* (1962),[15] James Buchanan and Gordon Tullock, *The Calculus of Consent* (1962),[16] Forrest McDonald, *E Pluribus Unum* (1965),[17] Edward Banfield, *The Unheavenly City* (1970),[18] Harvey Mansfield, *The Spirit of Liberalism* (1978),[19] George Gilder, *Wealth and Poverty* (1981),[20] Herbert Storing, *What the Anti-Federalists Were For* (1981),[21] Richard Neuhaus, *The Naked Public Square* (1984),[22] Charles Murray, *Losing Ground* (1984),[23] Allan Bloom, *The Closing of the American Mind* (1987),[24] E. D. Hirsch, *Cultural Literacy* (1987),[25] and Shelby Steele, *The Content of Our Character* (1991).[26]

The titles alone illustrate the breadth and division of conservatism's competing interests, which Ronald Reagan had to balance in his efforts to popularize conservatism and convert it into an effective political message that could successfully do battle with the powerful forces of modern liberalism.

The Wings of Modern Conservatism

In the modern era, five distinct wings of the conservative movement, both intellectually and politically, emerged from this diverse flowering of conservative thought just described: neoconservatives, libertarians, Midwestern conservatives, traditionalists, and religious conservatives. Ronald Reagan blended all of these schools of conservative thought in his successful effort to advance the popular cause of conservatism. Although distinctive, the five wings overlap and influence one another because they possess several common interests.

Neoconservatives—former liberals perhaps best personified by venerable figures such as Irving Kristol and Norman Podhoretz—began to take refuge under the conservative tent during the late 1960s and early 1970s. Disaffected by liberalism's increasing fondness during that era for a weaker military and greatly enlarged social programs, neoconservatives found themselves attracted to the conservative ideals of nationalism and a slower rate of social change. But geographically located primarily in the Northeast, particularly New York City, they do not share the same religious and cultural convictions as many of those conservatives who live in the South, Midwest, and Sunbelt states.

Libertarians appear to their critics to be chameleons; they certainly cannot be categorized easily as either conventional liberals or conservatives. On one hand, they ardently advocate autonomy of the individual, a minimal role for government, and a vibrant free-market economy. But on the other, they often oppose governmental action to limit or ban abortion, measures to allow school prayer, and other initiatives supported by traditional conservatives, who argue that libertarians, by placing undue emphasis on liberty, embrace a form of unbridled individualism that fails to respect community customs and traditions.

Midwestern conservatives often differ from other conservatives, particularly those in the South and Sunbelt. Laying claim to the pragmatic mantle of Abraham Lincoln, they are less ideological and more prone to compromise, as illustrated by the legislative leadership provided by many among their ranks over the decades, including Senators Robert A. Taft, Everett McKinley Dirksen and Robert Dole, and President Gerald Ford. Political philosophy guides but does not govern Midwestern conservatism, unlike the emergent conservative leaders from the South and Sunbelt, symbolized best by Newt Gingrich. For pragmatic and humanitarian reasons, Midwestern conservatives may even promote policies that would enlarge the size and scope of the national government. Thus, Senator Taft advocated public housing during the late 1940s, while Senator Dirksen provided the absolutely essential support needed to pass the Civil Rights Act of 1964 and the Voting Rights Act of 1965.

Traditionalist conservatives, often called paleoconservatives, look to thinkers like Richard Weaver, Russell Kirk, and the Southern Agrarians for intellectual guidance. Traditionalists once stood in the vanguard of the modern conservative movement, providing substantial intellectual leadership over several decades, beginning especially during the 1940s. On the home front, they reacted to excesses of liberalism in American society, brought about by a greatly enlarged national government through the New Deal, Fair Deal, New Frontier, and Great Society. And on the foreign front, they boldly spoke out against the threat of utopian communism. Their leaders included the aforementioned Russell Kirk, William F. Buckley, Robert Nisbet, and many others.

Religious conservatives are in many ways the first cousins or fraternal twins of traditional conservatives. For example, they share a common concern about the breakdown in America's social order. But religious conservatives, who include evangelical Christians, conservative Roman Catholics, most Mormons, and some Jews, express particular disdain for the rise of abortion, homosexuality, and other affronts to their religious heretics. Their intellectual and political leaders include such figures as Stanley Jaki, author of *The Absolute Beneath the Relative* (1988), and Francis Schaeffer, author of *How Should We Then Live?* (1983), James Dobson of Focus on the Family, and William Donohue of the Catholic League.

Conservatism and the Challenge of the Post-Reagan Era

Ronald Reagan rode the power of this diverse intellectual and political coalition to victory in 1980, promising the country an alternative to failures liberalism's at home and its defeatist appeasement of global communism abroad. Reagan was a true master in delivering in concrete and rhetorical ways the political goods that each of the distinct wings of his electoral coalition desired. For neoconservative and other anticommunist nationalists, Reagan provided an unprecedented military build-up to fight and defeat the forces and proxies of Soviet communism. For libertarians and pro-business Republicans, he pushed through a 30 percent across-the-board tax cut, regulatory relief, and reductions in domestic discretionary spending. For Midwestern conservatives, he delivered opposition to affirmative action, anti-crime legislation, and consistent rhetorical flourishes extolling the merits of American exceptionalism and patriotism. And for traditionalist and religious conservatives, Reagan saved up originalist judges, anti-abortion political appointees, and the rhetoric of family values.

Since the passing of Ronald Reagan, no political leader has emerged who could so adroitly balance conservatism's deep philosophical and political divisions while also responding effectively to new realities and challenges.

Of course, one of the new realities conservatives face today is a product of Reagan's success—the passing of Soviet communism into the dustbin of history. Opposition to communism—its atheism, utopianism, statism, and expansionism—was truly the glue that kept all of the wings of the postwar conservative coalition together. Without it, today there is far less to unite, for example, traditionalist conservatives and libertarians, and as the current efforts to combat global terrorism and rogue regimes demonstrate, these contemporary enemies have done more to divide conservatives than to bring them together. Needless to say, these are different times than when Reagan's brand of anticommunist nationalism fused the disparate wings of American conservatism into a united political force.

In addition to new geopolitical realities, there have emerged other distinct challenges to a developed conservative worldview. Among these challenges is postmodernism, which through an ironizing of language and meaning especially undermines conservatism's desire for order and stability. In his ten-volume *Study of History*, Arnold Toynbee concluded that civilizations rarely collapse from conquest or invasion, but rather typically fall through a form of cultural suicide, abandoning their inherited beliefs for something—almost anything—new.[27] Culturally, nothing is more important than language; words provide coherence and cohesion to society, relating to one another and collectively shaping the significance of reality and defining the meaning of life. When words lose consistent and coherent meaning, they no longer serve as dependable points of reference or anchors of stability.[28]

But there are other challenges as well, some of them related to our postmodern condition, as the contributors to this volume make clear. In the pages that follow, some of today's most insightful conservative scholars, writers, and pundits examine the major issues that confront twenty-first-century conservatism. They address such matters as:

- Ronald Reagan's conservative character and leadership legacy;
- the economic, philosophical, political, religious, and social impact of conservatism on American society;
- divisions, tensions, and critical problems facing American conservatism; and
- the impact of contemporary American foreign policy on the unity of the conservative coalition.

As these authors demonstrate, conservatism's strength has always rested in the realm of ideas, which fueled the fire of the so-called "Reagan Revolution." So long as conservatism emphasizes philosophy over the realm of pragmatism and politics, it will have a formidable future. Serving as the principal political instrument for the advancement of conservative thought, Ronald Reagan understood the truth alluded to by the title of Richard Weaver's classic book, *Ideas Have Consequences*.[29] Ideas endure, politicians change. Contemporary conservatives of all persuasions would be wise to heed that crucial insight.

I

The Uneasy Future of American Conservatism

George H. Nash

IN THE BOISTEROUS CHATTER of current political debate, it is easy to forget that American conservatism has become middle-aged. In 2005 its flagship publication, National Review, celebrated its fiftieth anniversary. A couple of years before that, the Intercollegiate Studies Institute, another star in the conservative firmament, celebrated its own half-century of existence, along with the golden anniversary of Russell Kirk's tour de force, *The Conservative Mind*. In Washington, DC, the Heritage Foundation—the nerve center of the conservative public policy establishment—is now more than thirty years old.

The Anxieties of Maturity

What happens when a political movement reaches maturity? For those within its ranks, the impulse grows to proclaim success and salute its intrepid founders in festschrifts, biographies, and other acts of commemoration. For those outside its ranks, passion yields to envious curiosity: how, the critics wonder, did such a phenomenon come into prominence and power? With the advent of middle age, present-mindedness gives way slowly to increased self-consciousness and a quest for deeper understanding of one's roots.

In 2007 American conservatives are proudly conscious of their past. But mingling with their impulse to celebrate is a discernible note of unease. In part this is a consequence of the instability of the world as we now know it. Particularly since September 11, 2001, Americans of all political persuasions have lived with a heightened sense of the unpredictability of events. Whether the source of anxiety be terrorism abroad, hurricanes at home, the prospect of nuclear weaponry in the hands of Iran, or predictions of an imminent global pandemic of bird flu, many Americans at present are convinced that things are not quite under control. All this makes it risky for anyone in politics to rest on his laurels. Relaxation is impossible. The shape of the future cannot be taken for granted.

Other unsettling perceptions are peculiar to conservatives. Among many on the right, there is a growing realization that conservatism's political success in recent decades has not been matched by commensurate changes in the way we live. For two generations the critique of the liberal welfare state has been integral to conservative discourse, yet governmental expenditures and regulations continue to grow. Conservatives passionately decry the tide of moral relativism, yet year by year they perceive a further hollowing out of the moral foundations of our civilization. There is a sense, moreover, in parts of the conservative intellectual community, that "the old gray mare, she ain't what she used to be": that the conservative movement itself has been corrupted, even transmogrified, on its road to power.

Lurking beneath these anxieties is another, seldom expressed yet not far (one suspects) from the surface of conservative consciousness: when a political or intellectual movement becomes middle-aged, does this mean that its glory days are numbered? Must noonday sunshine fade inevitably into twilight? To put it bluntly: is the sun about to set on the conservative empire?

The Evolution of Fusion

Such questions cannot be addressed in a vacuum. Before we can profitably peer into conservatism's future, it is necessary to grasp its present configuration and understand how the present came to be. In a post-9/11 world, it would be a bold person indeed who would venture to predict the contingent factors that may affect the prospects of American conservatives. In this respect the future is unknowable. What *is* knowable is conservatism's past. By examining the recent evolution of the American Right, we can identify some of the internal factors that impinge upon its present, creating the frontier where the next chapter in the conservative saga will be written. In conservatism's own history, first as an intellectual and then as a political movement, may be found important clues to its problematic present and uncertain future.

Perhaps the most important fact to assimilate about modern American conservatism is that it is not, and has never been, univocal. It is a *coalition* with

2

many points of origin and diverse tendencies, not always easy to reconcile: a river of thought and activism fed by many tributaries. At its best it has been driven not by petty material interests but by ideas and by a driving urge to implement them. It is a coalition, moreover, that has evolved over two generations: a datum of increasing significance.

In 1945, at the close of World War II, no articulate, coordinated conservative intellectual force existed in the United States. There were, at most, scattered voices of protest, profoundly pessimistic about the future of their country and convinced that they were an isolated Remnant, standing athwart history yelling, in the words of William F. Buckley Jr. at *National Review*, "Stop!" History, in fact, seemed to be what the Left was making. The Left—liberals, socialists, even communists—appeared to be in complete control of the twentieth century.

In the beginning, in the aftermath of the war, there was not one right-wing renaissance but three, each reacting in diverse ways to challenge from the Left. The first of these groupings consisted of libertarians and classical liberals, resisting the threat of the ever-expanding State to individual liberty, free-market capitalism, and individual initiative in the economic realm. Convinced in the 1940s that post–New Deal America was rapidly drifting toward central planning and socialism—toward what the economist Friedrich Hayek famously called "the road to serfdom"—these intellectuals offered a powerful defense of free-market economics that achieved some prominence and influence by the mid-1950s. From men like Hayek, Ludwig von Mises, and John Chamberlain in the 1940s and 1950s, to Milton Friedman and the Chicago School economists in the 1960s, to Arthur Laffer and the supply-side economists in the 1980s, and to such recent winners of the Nobel Prize in Economics as Gary Becker, the libertarian conservatives produced a sophisticated defense of free-market capitalism and exerted an enormous influence over the American Right. They helped to make the old verities defensible again after the long nightmare of the Great Depression. The Reagan administration's policies of tax-rate cutting, deregulation, and encouragement of private-sector economic growth in the 1980s were the direct product of this intellectual legacy. More recently, the current Bush administration's agenda for tax-cutting can be traced intellectually to the supply-side orthodoxy that captured the Republican Party in the Reagan era.

Much of this perspective was enunciated in powerful books, such as Hayek's masterly polemic *The Road to Serfdom* (1944), a book now recognized as one of the most influential works published in the English language in the twentieth century. Other works of note included Ludwig von Mises' *Human Action* (1949), Milton Friedman's bestselling *Capitalism and Freedom* (1962), Thomas Sowell's *Knowledge and Decisions* (1980), and George Gilder's

Wealth and Poverty (1981). On a more popular level, the free-market fiction of Ayn Rand shaped the minds of many, including a young man named Alan Greenspan.

Concurrently, and independently of the libertarians, a second school of nonliberal thought emerged in America in the first decade after World War II: the "new conservatism" or "traditionalism" of such men as Richard Weaver, Peter Viereck, Robert Nisbet, and Russell Kirk. Appalled by totalitarianism, total war, and the development of secular, rootless, mass society during the 1930s and 1940s, the "new conservatives" (as they were then called) urged a return to traditional religious and ethical absolutes and a rejection of the moral relativism that had allegedly corroded Western values and produced an intolerable vacuum filled by demonic ideologies. More European-oriented and historically minded, on the whole, than the classical liberals, the traditionalist conservatives extolled the wisdom of such thinkers as Edmund Burke, Alexis de Tocqueville, and the Anglo-American literary giant T. S. Eliot, and called for a revival of Christian orthodoxy, classical natural law, pre-modern political philosophy, and mediating institutions between the citizen and the state. Why? In order, they said, to reclaim and civilize the spiritual wasteland created by secular liberalism and the false gods it had permitted to enter the gates.

In provocative books like Richard Weaver's *Ideas Have Consequences* (1948) and Robert Nisbet's *The Quest for Community* (1953), the traditionalists expounded a vision of a healthy and virtuous society antithetical to the tenets of contemporary liberalism. From towering European émigré scholars like Leo Strauss and Eric Voegelin they learned new techniques for assessing the problem of secular modernity. From Russell Kirk's monumental tome *The Conservative Mind* (1953) the fledgling traditionalists acquired something more: an intellectual genealogy and intellectual respectability. After Kirk's book appeared, no longer could conservatism be dismissed, as John Stuart Mill had dismissed British conservatives a century before, as "the stupid party." No longer could conservatism be disparaged as the philosophy of provincials and philistines. In books like *The Conservative Mind* the highbrow conservative academics of the 1950s struck a blow against the liberals' superiority complex.

Third, there appeared in the 1940s and 1950s, at the onset of the Cold War, a militant, evangelistic anticommunism, shaped by a number of ex-communists and ex-Trotskyists of the 1930s, including Whittaker Chambers, James Burnham, Frank Meyer, and many more. It was also reinforced by anticommunist exiled scholars from Eastern and Central Europe, including Stefan Possony and Gerhart Niemeyer. These former men and women of the Left and their European émigré allies brought to the postwar American Right a profound conviction that America and the West were engaged in a titanic struggle with an implacable adversary—communism—which sought nothing less than the conquest of the world.

Each of these emerging components of the conservative revival shared a deep antipathy to twentieth-century liberalism. To the libertarians, modern liberalism—the liberalism of Franklin Roosevelt and his successors—was the ideology of the ever aggrandizing, bureaucratic welfare state which would, if unchecked, become a centralized totalitarian state, destroying individual liberty and private property. To the traditionalists, modern liberalism was a disintegrative philosophy which, like an acid, was eating away not only at our liberties but also at the ethical and institutional foundations of traditional society, thereby creating a vast spiritual vacuum into which totalitarianism could enter. To the Cold War anticommunists, modern liberalism—rationalistic, relativistic, secular, anti-traditional, quasi-socialist—was by its very nature incapable of vigorously resisting an enemy on its Left. Liberalism to them was *part* of the Left and could not effectively repulse a foe with which it shared so many underlying assumptions. As James Burnham eventually and trenchantly put it, modern liberalism was essentially a means for reconciling the West to its own destruction. Liberalism was the ideology of Western suicide.

In the late 1950s and early 1960s the three independent wings of the conservative revolt against the Left began to coalesce. The movement found its first popular embodiment in the editor of *National Review*, William F. Buckley Jr., who, apart from his extraordinary talents, personified each impulse in the developing coalition. He was at once a traditional Roman Catholic, a defender of the free market, and a staunch anticommunist (a source of his ecumenical appeal to conservatives.

The Evolution of Division

As this consolidation began to occur, certain intellectual problems arose for those who took the name conservative. It was not enough for them to rebel against contemporary liberalism. If they were conservatives, what did they wish to conserve? What was the conservative tradition to which they professed such fealty?

It soon transpired that the conservative intellectuals (not all of whom liked the word "conservative") gave a variety of answers. Some identified conservatism with the defense of Christian orthodoxy. Some extolled what they labeled the Great Tradition of political philosophy going back to ancient Greece and Rome. Some invoked natural law in opposition to liberalism's emphasis on natural rights. Some venerated Edmund Burke as their political patron saint. Most admired America's Founding Fathers and its tradition of limited government and constitutionalism. Some, like Hayek, repudiated the conservative label entirely and styled themselves Old Whigs or classical liberals.

Complicating this quest for philosophical order was a severe challenge to the fragile conservative identity: a growing and permanent tension between the libertarians and the traditionalists. To the libertarians the highest good in society was individual liberty, the emancipation of the autonomous self from external (especially governmental) restraint. To the traditionalists (who tended to be more religiously oriented than most libertarians) the highest social good was not unqualified freedom but decent behavior, or, as they often put it, *ordered* freedom resting ultimately on the cultivation of virtue in the individual soul. Such cultivation, argued traditionalists, did not arise spontaneously. It needed the reinforcement and guidance of mediating institutions and even of the government itself. To put it another way, libertarians tended to believe in the beneficence of an uncoerced and spontaneous social order, both in markets and morals. The traditionalists often agreed, more or less, about the market order, but they were far less sanguine about the unregulated moral order. Spontaneity was not a term of endearment in the traditionalist lexicon.

Not surprisingly, this conflict of visions generated a tremendous polemical controversy on the American Right in the 1960s, as conservative intellectuals attempted to sort out their first principles. The argument became known as the freedom-versus-virtue debate. It fell to a former communist and chief ideologist at *National Review*, a man named Frank Meyer, to formulate a middle way that became known as fusionism—that is, a fusing or reconciliation of the competing paradigms of the "libs" and the "trads." As a purely theoretical construct, Meyer's fusionism was rickety, but as a formula for political action and as an insight into the actual character of American conservatism, Meyer's project was a considerable success. He taught libertarian and traditionalist purists that they needed each other and that American conservatism must not become doctrinaire. To be relevant and influential, especially politically, it must stand neither for an abstract, dogmatic antistatism nor for a regimenting authoritarianism but for a society in which people are simultaneously free to choose and desirous of choosing the path of virtue.

In arriving at this modus vivendi, the architects of fusionism were aided immensely by the third element in the developing coalition: anticommunism, an ideology that everyone could share. The presence in the world of a dangerous external enemy—the Soviet Union, the Evil Empire, the mortal foe of liberty *and* virtue, of freedom *and* faith—was a crucial cement for the nascent conservative movement. The life-and-death stakes of the Cold War helped to curb the temptation of right-wing ideologues to absolutize their competing insights and thereby commit heresy.

Politically, the postwar American Right found its first national expression in the campaign of Senator Barry Goldwater for the presidency of the United States in 1964. The 1964 election had three enduring consequences for conservatives. It created the Democratic congressional majorities which permitted enactment of President Lyndon Johnson's Great Society program, the greatest lurch to the Left in domestic policy since the New Deal. It led to conservative capture of the political machinery of the Republican Party. And it created a new national political figure in Ronald Reagan, whose eloquent television speech for Goldwater on the eve of the election led directly to Reagan's successful candidacy for governor of California two years later.

It was not long after the 1964 election that a new impulse appeared on the intellectual-political scene, one destined to become the fourth component of today's conservative coalition. The phenomenon became known as neoconservatism. Irving Kristol's definition conveyed its essence. A neoconservative, he said, was "a liberal who has been mugged by reality." According to another definition, a neoconservative was someone who uttered two cheers for capitalism instead of three. In any case, one of the salient developments of the late 1960s and 1970s was the intellectual journey of various liberals and social democrats toward conservative positions.

The stresses that produced this migration were many. In part, neoconservatism may be interpreted as the recognition by disillusioned denizens of the Left that good intentions alone do not guarantee good governmental policy and that the actual consequences of liberal social activism in the sixties and seventies were often devastating. In this context, it is clear that one of the key intellectual events of the 1960s was the founding of The *Public Interest* in 1965, an act of revisionist liberalism that forced many melioristic social scientists to reexamine their premises. In considerable measure neoconservatism was also a reaction of moderate liberals to the antinomian cultural upheavals of the 1960s, particularly on the college and university campuses, and to the eruption of the so-called New Left, with its tendency to blame America first for world tensions and its neoisolationist hostility to a vigorous prosecution of the Cold War.

Many neoconservatives, in fact, were former anticommunist liberals of the Harry Truman/Henry Jackson wing of the Democratic Party who found themselves bereft of a political home after the capture of their party by the followers of George McGovern in 1972. Such names as Irving Kristol, Norman Podhoretz (the editor of *Commentary*), and Midge Decter come quickly to mind.

To the already existing conservative community, the entry of erstwhile liberals and socialists into its precincts was to have many consequences. One of these was already discernible in the 1970s. Since the days of the New

Deal, American liberals had held a near monopoly on the manufacture and distribution of prestige among the intellectual and chattering classes. From a liberal perspective, the libertarian, traditionalist, and Cold War conservatives of the fifties and sixties were eccentric figures, no threat to liberalism's cultural hegemony.

The emerging neoconservatives, however, were an "enemy within" who had made their reputations while still on the left and could not be so easily dismissed. By publicly defecting from the Left, and by critiquing it so effectively, the neoconservatives undermined a hitherto unshakable assumption in academic circles: the belief that only liberalism is an intellectually respectable point of view. By destroying the automatic equation of liberalism with intelligence, the neoconservative intellectuals brought new respectability to the Right and greatly altered the terms of public debate in the United States.

Meanwhile another development—one destined to have enormous political consequences—began to take shape in the late 1970s: the political "great awakening" of what came to be known as the Religious Right. Initially the Religious Right was not primarily a movement of intellectuals at all. It was, rather, a groundswell of protest at the grassroots of America by aroused citizens, many of them Protestant evangelicals, fundamentalists, and pentecostals, but including some Roman Catholics and Orthodox Jews as well. While Religious Right leaders like Jerry Falwell, Pat Robertson, and James Dobson appeared to share the foreign policy and economic perspectives of earlier conservatives, their guiding preoccupations lay elsewhere, in what became known as the "social issues": abortion, school prayer, pornography, drug use, sexual deviancy, the vulgarization of mass entertainment, and more. Convinced that American society was in a state of vertiginous moral decline, and that what they called secular humanism—in other words, modern or postmodern liberalism—was the fundamental cause of this decay, the Religious Right exhorted its hitherto politically quiescent followers to enter the public arena in defense of their traditional moral code and way of life.

In a very real sense the Religious Right was closest in its concerns to traditionalist conservatism. The Religious Right also shared the neoconservatives' revulsion against the nihilism of the sixties. But whereas the traditionalists of the 1940s and 1950s had largely been academics in revolt *against* rootless, mass society, the Religious Right of the 1980s was a revolt *by* the "masses" against the secular virus and its carriers in the nation's elites. And whereas the traditionalist conservatives of the pre-Reagan era had been disproportionately Roman Catholic and the neoconservatives disproportionately Jewish, the religious conservatives who became prominent in the Reagan era were disproportionately drawn from the ranks of long marginalized evangelical Protestants.

8

And whereas conservative intellectuals had heretofore concentrated most of their energies on national issues (like economic policy and conduct of the Cold War), the Religious Right was different. It addressed the moral traumas experienced by ordinary people in their everyday lives, especially those conflicts affecting the transmission of normative values to the young. Above all, the religious conservatives derived their fervor from an unremitting struggle against what most of them considered the supreme abomination of their time: legalized abortion, a practice that from 1973 to the present has taken the lives of more than 40 million unborn children.

In time the Religious Right acquired intellectually influential voices. Many other conservative writers shared its disquietude about the debasement and de-moralization of culture and joined in various struggles to reverse the tide. The phenomenon gained further momentum from its organic ties to a vast and growing evangelical Protestant subculture: a "parallel universe" (as one observer has called it) of Christian universities, colleges, television and radio stations, magazines, publishing houses, philanthropies, parachurch ministries, crisis pregnancy centers, and bookstores. It acquired still more influence by forging an alliance with like-minded Roman Catholics and Orthodox Jews—a conservative ecumenical movement without precedent in American history.

Ronald Reagan and the Triumph of Ecumenicity

Spearheaded at the political level by the Moral Majority and then by the Christian Coalition, the Religious Right brought to American conservatism a moral intensity and populist dimension not seen since the Goldwater campaign of 1964, indeed transcending it. By the end of President Reagan's second term in office, the American Right had grown to encompass five distinct impulses: libertarianism, traditionalism, anticommunism, neoconservatism, and the interfaith Religious Right. And just as William F. Buckley Jr. had done for intellectual conservatives a generation before, so Ronald Reagan in the 1980s performed an ecumenical function politically, giving each faction a seat at the table and a sense of having arrived.

Reagan also did something more. As Michael Barone has recently observed, the Great Communicator gave American conservatism a demotic voice and a more optimistic tone, evoking hope for the future rather than nostalgia for the past. In the dark days of the 1940s and early 1950s, American conservatives had occasionally sounded like General Bullmoose in the Broadway play *L'il Abner*: "Progress is the root of all evil / Bring back the good old days!" Reagan's message more nearly resembled the motto of the General Electric Company (for which he had worked as spokesman in the 1950s): "Progress is our most important product." More than any conservative leader in memory, he reaffirmed the continuing validity and vitality of the American Dream.

With Reagan's political triumph as a clinching incentive, American conservatism completed a transition, already underway in the 1960s, from a defiant, contrarian, minority posture and rhetoric to a confident identification with Middle America. Conservatives who had once perceived themselves as history's losers now saw themselves as the vanguard of the silent majority. With Reagan's presidential candidacy providing the bridge, both the neoconservatives and the Religious Right crossed the Rubicon into the arms of the conservative coalition.

As these disparate elements merged under Reagan into a political as well as intellectual force, they experienced a stirring passage from the world of theory to the world of public policy. Perhaps the most striking feature of conservative intellectual activity in the Age of Reagan was that there was so much of it. The publication of conservative books, articles, and syndicated columns— already substantial in the 1970s—attained in the Reagan era the proportions of an avalanche. Gone were the days when *National Review* and a couple of other periodicals constituted the virtual totality of intelligent conservative journalism in the United States. Increasingly, it seemed that every strand of the conservative movement had its own publication—its own branch, as it were, on the family tree.

This cascade of literature was intimately linked to a second extraordinary trend: the proliferation of a burgeoning network of conservative media, foundations, research centers, and idea-based advocacy groups, from the shores of the Potomac to the farthest corners of the country. By the 1990s literally hundreds of them had come into being. In the legal profession, a phalanx of public interest law firms challenged overweening government in the courts. Among law students and legal scholars, the Federalist Society (founded in 1982) articulated conservative approaches to constitutional interpretation and provided an invaluable resource for networking and information exchange. In the field of environmental policy the Political Economy Research Center (PERC), based in Bozeman, Montana, championed a paradigm shift known as free-market environmentalism. For Religious Right activists, the Focus on the Family organization, the Family Research Council, and the American Center for Law and Justice, among other groups, provided an arsenal of intellectual and legal ammunition.

The examples are legion, but the point is clear. Within a span of less than a generation, something truly remarkable occurred in American political and intellectual life: a vibrant conservative counterculture was forged. We need not dilate upon its more recent and familiar manifestations, such as the efflorescence of talk radio, the spread of homeschooling and classical Christian schools, and the birth of the blogosphere. Suffice it to note the magnitude of the change. No longer a tiny and marginalized Remnant, the conservative conglomerate as we know it today, Hillary Clinton's "vast right-wing conspiracy," is literally at our fingertips, if we but choose to tune in or log on.

Fueling this surge in programmatic conservatism was another development which the Reagan presidency accelerated: a deepening collaboration between conservative intellectuals and politicians. Such a symbiosis had long been common on the other side of the ideological spectrum. From the New Deal of Franklin Roosevelt to the New Frontier of John F. Kennedy to the Great Society of Lyndon Johnson, prominent academicians have regularly supplied "idea power" to the American Left. Since 1980 this "intellectualization" of domestic politics and public policy formulation has extended to the American Right as well.

There was no more dramatic example of this trend than the appearance in the 1970s of a body of thought called "supply-side economics," initially identified with Professor Arthur Laffer of the University of Southern California. In a remarkably short time Laffer's work was enthusiastically publicized by several influential conservative writers until, in the form of tax-reduction legislation sponsored by Representative Jack Kemp and Senator William Roth, it became the official tax policy of the Republican Party. In 1980 Ronald Reagan heartily endorsed this proposal, and he signed a modified form of it into law early in his presidency. No more could it be charged that conservative politicians were stodgy reactionaries lacking in fresh ideas. On the contrary, many of them— like Newt Gingrich, Steve Forbes, and Reagan himself—craved ideas, thrived on ideas, and found in supply-side economics a way of taking the ideological offensive. In supply-side economics, theory and practice decisively merged. The Republican Party has not been the same since.

The Ambiguities of Success and the Perils of Prosperity

The successes of the Reagan years did not come without costs, however. During the 1980s and long afterwards, conservative intellectuals (usually of a traditionalist bent) could be heard to complain at times that the conservative cause was being "reduced to politics," drained of its ethical vision, and deflected from its larger mission of cultural renewal. As the Reagan Revolution passed into history some of its intellectual architects—especially libertarians— wondered what it had really accomplished. Reagan had tarnished the intellectual pretensions of social democracy, to be sure, and had undermined the legitimacy of the liberal status quo. But he had not overturned it; "big government" was bigger than ever.

More recently, scholars such as Steven Hayward have noted that the rise of "populist" or majoritarian conservatism in the eighties (and beyond) was accompanied by a conspicuous weakening of the antistatist ideology that had long united conservatives. Still others have suggested that conservative politics, like all politics, attracts not only those who come to do good but also those who come to do well. Conservative journalist M. Stanton Evans has famously remarked that over the years some conservatives have gone to Washington believing it to be a cesspool, only to decide that it is really a hot tub.

From the perspective of today it is increasingly apparent that the Reagan presidency coincided with and fostered a profound, generational shift in American conservatism. Before 1980 the American Right had been primarily a movement of dissent, spearheaded by intellectuals. Its capital city (to the extent that it had one) was New York, the home of *National Review*. After 1980 it became a political movement as well, subject to the constraints and temptations of political action. Its capital city, the focus of its dreams and energies, became Washington, DC, itself. Perhaps not coincidentally, in practice if not quite in theory American conservatism today stands well to the left of where it stood in 1980.

Yet even as conservatives in the eighties and nineties escaped the wilderness for the promised land inside the Beltway, the world they wished to conquer was changing in ways that threatened their newfound power. Ask yourself this question: aside from conservatism, what have been the most important social movements in America in the past thirty years? To this historian the answer is plain: feminism and environmentalism. Since the 1970s the United States has been moving right *and* left at the same time. Out in the culture—both highbrow and lowbrow—the vectors of social change have not been pointing in a uniformly conservative direction.

Next, ask yourself this: what has been the most historically consequential date for conservatives in the past generation? September 11, 2001? Perhaps. But surely the other such date was November 9, 1989, the night that the Berlin Wall came down. Since 1989 one of the hallmarks of conservative history has been the reappearance of factional strains in the grand alliance.

By far the most persistent source of discontent on the right has been the status within its ranks of the neoconservatives. To an angry group of traditionalists in the late 1980s who took the label "paleoconservatives," the "neocons" were "interlopers," "impostors," and Johnny-come-latelies who, despite their recent journey to the right, remained essentially secular, Wilsonian, and welfare-statist in their underlying philosophy. In other words, said their critics, they were not truly conservative at all. During the final phase of the Cold War, and more recently during the war against Islamist terrorism, the paleocons accused the neocons of foisting on the Right a profoundly unconservative, neo-Wilsonian ideology of "global democratic capitalism." As if, said disgusted paleocons like Patrick Buchanan, Wilsonian "global democracy" were the sum and substance of the conservative vision.

Like the neoconservatives against whom it endlessly polemicized, pugnacious paleoconservatism became a discordant element in conservative circles. Fiercely and defiantly "nationalist" (rather than "internationalist"), skeptical of "global democracy" and entanglements overseas, and fearful of the impact of Third World immigration on America's Eurocentric culture, Buchananite paleoconservatism increasingly resembled much of the American Right *before* 1945; before, that is, the onset of the Cold War. When Buchanan himself campaigned for the presidency in 1992 under the pre–World War II, anti-interventionist banner of "America First," the symbolism seemed deliberate and complete.

Nor were neoconservatives the only faction to come under fire from disaffected members of the pre-Reagan Right. To certain libertarians and traditionalists, it appeared that the other latecomer to the coalition, the Religious Right, was also insufficiently antistatist—too willing to use governmental power to implement its moral vision. Congressional intervention in the Terry Schiavo case in 2005 brought some of these latent conflicts to the surface.

Aside from the built-in philosophical tensions with which the conservative coalition has been living for half a century, two fundamental facts of political life explain the recrudescence of intramural debates among conservatives since the Reagan era. The first is what we might call the perils of prosperity. In the 1950s and early 1960s the number of publicly active, conservative intellectuals in the United States was minuscule: perhaps a few dozen at most. Today how can one even begin to conduct such a count? Prosperity has come to conservatism, and with it a multitude of niche markets and specialization on a thousand fronts. With prosperity and specialization have also come signs of sibling rivalry and an attenuation of "movement consciousness," as the various elements in the coalition pursue their separate agendas.

Although the Heritage Foundation and others have taken important steps to coordinate conservative activism inside the Beltway, the "vast right-wing conspiracy" is now so large and dispersed that no single institution can function as its general staff, as *National Review* was able to do in its early days. No longer does American conservatism have a commanding ecumenical figure like Buckley or Reagan.

As the conservative universe has expanded, there has arisen a tendency to categorize conservatives in ever smaller subgroups. Thus we have the neocons, the paleocons, the "theocons" (theological or religious conservatives), and the "Leocons" (disciples of Leo Strauss or Straussians). Certain immigrant conservative writers like David Frum and John O'Sullivan have been dubbed "immicons." Traditionalist conservatives with "green" sensibilities and countercultural tastes are called "crunchy cons." Young conservatives have been labeled "minicons." All this is rather playful and amusing, but it does suggest the sectarian impulses at work.

The second fundamental fact of political life that explains the renewal of friction on the right is one that has been hinted at already. It did not escape notice in the early 1990s that the conservatives' uncivil strife coincided with the dismantling of the Berlin Wall, the collapse of communism in Europe, and the stunning end of the Cold War. Until then most conservatives had been governed by Benjamin Franklin's prudential advice in 1776: "We must all hang together, or assuredly we shall all hang separately."

Inevitably, after 1989, the question arose: could a movement so identified with unyielding anticommunism survive the disappearance of the adversary in the Kremlin? Or would long-suppressed centrifugal tendencies prevail?

The Challenge of William Jefferson Clinton

The conservative movement, of course, did not crumble in the 1990s. Predictions of its imminent demise proved unfounded. Conservatism since 1945, after all, had always encompassed more than geopolitical anticommunism. The downfall of the Soviet Union did not render obsolete the deeper, civilizational concerns of a Friedrich Hayek, a Richard Weaver, or a Russell Kirk. Conservatives were also helped by the appearance in 1993 of a new unifying agent in the person of William Jefferson Clinton. Nevertheless, it is undeniable that anticommunism supplied much of the glue in the post-1945 conservative coalition and that the death of communism in Europe weakened the fusionist imperative for American conservatives. As the post–Cold War era settled in during the 1990s, many conservatives appeared to be searching for a new, post-anticommunist synthesis of their aspirations.

Indeed, much conservative intellectual activity in the past ten years or so can be interpreted as a succession of efforts to formulate a new fusionism for a new era. In the first term of President Clinton, we saw the rise of the "Leave Us Alone" coalition, united in its detestation of intrusive government, be it in the form of higher taxes, Hillary Clinton's health care plan, gun control, or subversion of private property rights. Its galvanizing principle was that of individual liberty—the libertarian paradigm. A little later, certain neoconservatives at the *Weekly Standard* propounded something called "national greatness" conservatism, an adumbration of the muscular foreign policy of George W. Bush. Bush himself, before he was elected president, expounded what he called "compassionate conservatism." It was among other things a deliberate rebuke of the antistatist thrust of the Leave Us Alone movement and the confrontational governing style of Speaker of the House Newt Gingrich, which Bush perceived as an electoral dead-end.

More recently, the metaphor of war—with its insistent summons to unity—has returned to conservative discourse. A new enemy has appeared in radical Islam, and with it a new raison d'être for conservatives. The reemergence of foreign threats at the center of public consciousness after 9/11, and after what Charles Krauthammer has called our decade-long "holiday from history," gave American conservatism a renewed sense of mission grounded on the bedrock principle of national security. In the global war on terrorism most American conservative intellectuals and grassroots activists found the functional equivalent for the Cold War against communism.

On the home front, the cohesion that was once supplied by anticommunism has increasingly come from another "war," one that seems ever more integral to conservative identity. This is the so-called culture war, pitting an alliance of Roman Catholics, evangelical Protestants, and Orthodox Jewish believers against a postmodern, post-Christian, even anti-Christian secular elite whom they perceive to be aggressively hostile to their deepest convictions. Every day fresh tremors break out along this fault line—over abortion, euthanasia, gay marriage, stem-cell research, the Terry Schiavo case, "the war against Christmas," and the composition of the federal courts. It is a struggle literally over the meaning of right and wrong, a battle (for conservatives) against what Pope Benedict XVI has called "the tyranny of relativism." It is a protracted and seemingly irrepressible conflict that gives few signs of ebbing, at least among the media and political classes for whom politics seems increasingly to be a form of warfare.

The Challenge of George W. Bush

Whatever its outcome, for the present the conduct of the "culture war" has given most conservatives a renewed sense of purpose and embattlement. Yet all is not well on the Potomac. For a full generation now, American conservatism has thrived as a coalition of five distinct components, each reacting to a perceived external challenge from the Left. Now, for the first time in its history, conservatism confronts an *internal* challenge from an utterly unexpected source: the so-called "transformative" presidency of George W. Bush.

For the Religious Right and the neoconservatives, the Bush years have been relatively congenial ones. The president himself, a born-again Christian from Texas, has assiduously cultivated the Religious Right and has rewarded it with Supreme Court nominations and various public policy initiatives. To this crucial constituency he has appeared to be "one of us." Together with the Religious Right, many neoconservatives have exerted a powerful influence on the Bush administration's foreign policies and, just as importantly, on the rhetorical and theoretical garb with which they have been clothed. The editor of *First Things* has even suggested that the pro-life Religious Right and the neoconservatives have become the new center of gravity in the conservative coalition, vessels for a "new fusionism" aimed at remoralizing American life and foreign policy.

Other and older parts of the conservative coalition have been more ambivalent and at times dismayed. Although happy enough with the administration's judicial appointments and tax-cutting policies, they note that, under Bush, Medicare drug benefits have been expanded, educational policy has been increasingly nationalized, and federal spending (at least until recently) has been allowed to soar unchecked. For conservatives whose intellectual roots predate the 1980s, and for whom "limited government" has been a defining mantra, Washington, DC, in 2007 is not a pretty sight. Although "big government" conservatism—or, as they might say, big-government "conservatism"—may now be on the wane (at least in theory), it is painfully clear that a substantial segment of the American electorate has a vested interest in the welfare state and that anything deemed to be a frontal assault upon it is unlikely to be very successful.

Even more than its sometimes heterodox domestic policies, the Bush administration's approach to foreign affairs—especially in Iraq—has placed new stresses on the conservative coalition. The president's audacious assertion of executive power in the war on terrorism has rattled libertarians and others for whom the restraint of executive power is a settled conservative principle. His sweeping invocation of the language of democratic universalism reminds some conservatives of Eleanor Roosevelt—the epitome (for them) of platitudinous naïveté. For those who base their foreign policy outlook on the virtues of prudence and realism, Bush's "hard Wilsonianism" seems egregiously unconservative, although it must be added that, unlike Woodrow Wilson, Bush is not a supranationalist: a fact that has helped to draw conservative patriots to his colors.

With the exception of the paleoconservatives associated with Patrick Buchanan's *American Conservative* magazine, most conservatives, especially younger ones, continue to support Bush's conduct of the War on Terror, as the recent debate over national security wiretapping suggests. The seriousness of the terrorist threat, and the stridency and near hysteria of the antiwar Left, have done much to suppress any inclination on the right to defect from the man in the White House. But some "old school" conservative intellectuals, like George Carey and Jeffrey Hart, are now openly questioning whether the Bush administration is conservative at all. Like a pool player whose opening shot scatters the billiard balls in all directions, the president has unsettled many parts of his putative base. Whether the voices of dissent on the right grow louder will probably depend on contingent events in the Middle East and Asia.

The Future of a Fractious Coalition

And so we come to the uneasy future of American conservatism. It will be uneasy, first, because the global village in which we live is a troubled place, capable of altering the trajectory of our politics in unpredictable ways. It will be uneasy, secondly, because American conservatism, as it has evolved over two generations, is fundamentally a coalition—which, like all coalitions, contains within itself the potential for its own dissolution.

There is no certainty, for example, that the Religious Right—the largest demographic bloc in the right-wing alliance—will remain mobilized at the level of intensity that has brought conservative victories at the polls in recent years. In 2004 white evangelical Protestants accounted for approximately one-quarter of the voters in the presidential election, and they voted overwhelmingly for Bush. One catalyst for their high turnout was the presence on the ballots in eleven states of initiatives to prohibit homosexual marriage. The existence of these ballot referenda presumably helped the president gain votes, but this is not a tactic than can be replicated at every election.

Will the religious conservatives—"the boots on the ground" of the conservative movement, as Richard Land of the Southern Baptist Convention has called them—remain in their present state of discipline and zeal? The Religious Right's agenda of moral reformation has not been easily translatable into public policy, as the "thirty-year war" over abortion abundantly attests. If, for instance, future Supreme Court decisions should thwart the religious conservatives, or should some of their foot soldiers grow weary and discouraged, enough of them might relapse into political passivity to tip the electoral balance against the Right.

Is the long foretold "conservative crackup" just around the corner? Conceivably—but it has not happened yet in fifty years. Despite the genuine (and perennial) risks of such an implosion, despite the inherent philosophical tensions and intramural squabbles that have marked its history, the disintegration of the American Right seems unlikely any time soon. For one thing, each wing of the movement has become thoroughly institutionalized. From the Beltway to the blogosphere, the clusters of purposeful energy (and funding) that social scientists call institutions continue to multiply and flourish. These are not the manifestations of a dying political army. And thanks to such weapons as e-mail, the Internet, and Rush Limbaugh, the permanent mobilization of "the boots on

17

the ground," an electronic Tammany Hall, so to speak, seems easier than ever.

A conservative crackup is also unlikely because signs of cultural renewal—or at least of hope—continue to appear. One sees it in the growing interest in Christian-oriented movies and in the multiplicity of faith-based initiatives seeking the remoralization of our society: "compassionate conservatism" at the hardy grassroots. One sees it in the rise of what one author has called a "missionary generation" of college students coming out of evangelical Protestant, Roman Catholic, and Orthodox Jewish institutions of higher learning. If the "return to religion" that is now taking place on America's campuses (even in the Ivy League) persists, in fifteen years America may be a much different nation.

Above all, the conservative coalition seems destined to endure because most of the external stimuli that goaded it into existence have not disappeared. In some respects, they have grown stronger. The Berlin Wall may be gone, and socialist economics may be discredited, but significant sectors of American society continue to move in directions antithetical to conservative beliefs. Particularly in the area of "lifestyles"—of drug use, sexual mores, acceptance of pornography, and taste in mass entertainment—popular attitudes and behavior have veered sharply in a permissive, even neopagan, direction in recent decades.

More than forty years ago the conservative theorist Frank Meyer proclaimed that "the Christian understanding of the nature and destiny of man, which is the foundation of Western civilization, is always and everywhere what conservatives strive to conserve." Not everyone will accept this formulation. But those who do must admit that large swatches of American life—such as the academy, the media, and the entertainment industry—have become increasingly indifferent, even antagonistic, to the Christian faith and worldview. For defenders of Judeo-Christian ethics—and that means most conservatives—there remains much work to do. There is still a potent enemy on the left.

This precarious state of affairs raises a question. Can a national house so deeply divided govern itself effectively? Can a regime flourish in which the Right dominates the election returns and the making of public policy while the Left dominates our underlying mores and cultural transmission belts? Whether conservatives can thrive indefinitely without victory in the *final* struggle—the contest for our culture—may be the great, unanswered question about American politics.

A number of years ago a young member of the British Conservative Party was campaigning for a seat in Parliament. At a public rally he zestfully defended the Tory platform and concluded: "These are our principles. If you do not like them, we have others!"

American conservatism in its middle age is a diverse movement with many principles, not always easily harmonized. For this reason it may appear to be an unstable coalition. But it has also proved remarkably resilient, united in part by overlapping aspirations and by a recurrent sense of mortal challenge from enemies at home and abroad.

For conservatives the wilderness years are long over. But the conservative ascendancy is incomplete, and tomorrow belongs automatically to no one. If the conservative coalition is to continue to prosper, it must remember the ecumenism of Reagan, resist the tendency to fragment, and avoid the temptation to retreat into a fatal passivity induced by disillusionment or despair. Let not the words of an unknown poet become conservatism's epitaph:

> On the plains of hesitation
> Bleach the bones of countless millions
> Who, at the dawn of victory,
> Sat down to rest,
> And, resting, died.

2

Four Heads and One Heart:
The Modern Conservative Movement

James W. Ceaser

I HAVE HEARD IT said humorously that contemporary American conservatism, known to be fraught with many serious internal tensions, is held together by two self-evident truths: Nancy Pelosi and Barbara Boxer. If, as is more appropriate, these personal references are discarded, the general point still remains. Much of the unity that is found among conservatives today stems from their shared antipathy to liberalism, which serves as the common heart that beats in the breast of the conservative movement. Were liberalism by some strange dispensation of providence to cease to exist tomorrow, conservatism as we know it would begin to break apart on the next day.

Conservatism: A Coalition of Four Heads

No shame attaches—or should—to relying in politics on the adhesive properties supplied by a common dislike. Ours is a vast country in which it is only by coalition that a movement can hope to achieve and maintain a majority. Conservatism has been constructed over the last generation, mostly since the election of Ronald Reagan, from a coalition of the willing made up of four heads. These heads, all connected to and drawing their lifeblood from the same heart, are usually identified as: traditionalist or paleoconservatism, neoconservatism, libertarianism, and the Religious Right.

Liberalism, too, is a kind of coalition. One need only have listened to Teddy Kennedy in full rant mode during the Samuel Alito confirmation hearings—during those rare hiatuses when Joe Biden stopped talking—to appreciate that dislike of the opposition is also a vital factor for liberals in sustaining their movement. But there is an important difference in the character of the two coalitions. Conservatism is intellectually far more heterogeneous. Its heads or parts came into existence at different times and under different circumstances, and they have never claimed to be guided by the same principles. Some of these parts initially either did not embrace, or even outright rejected, the label of conservatism, adopting it only later on and for practical reasons. Liberals, by contrast, like at least to think that they are inspired by the same set of ideals. One consequence for liberals is that when conflicts spring up among them, the contesting factions regard the others' errors as evidence of their deviation from the true path, or heresy. Conservatism is not schismatic, and this for a simple reason: its different parts have never operated under any illusion about an ultimate agreement on first principles. Older parts may accuse newer ones of trying to usurp the movement and of not being genuinely conservative, but they rarely charge them with heresy. Their sin is that they never possessed the right principles in the first place.

Critics of conservatism often depict its heterogeneity as a grave weakness. How often today do we hear liberal commentators, particularly those of a certain intellectual pretentiousness, trotting out a classic conservative source from one camp in order to admonish the positions taken by conservatives from another? This ploy invariably follows the same smug formula: "I should have thought that conservatives, above all, would be especially mindful of X," where X could be a scrupulous protection of civil liberties and privacy (as if safety and national security were not also a concern of conservatives), or never undertaking a foreign occupation or nation-building (as if a need to battle new kinds of challenges by new responses had never been recommended by any school of conservatism). In the view of its liberal critics, the four heads of conservatism make it into an obvious monster.

But conservatives, when they are able to step back from pursuing their internecine quarrels, see this creature in a different light. The intense debate among its talking heads challenges and sharpens thinking, and thereby helps to avert intellectual complacency, which is the death knell of any movement or party. Better four heads than none. Once upon a time, one would have had every right to speak of intellectual *diversity*. But today the word means something else; it refers to a lock-step adherence to a single viewpoint, supposedly made diverse by being espoused by persons of different skin colors, sexes, or sexual orientations, although usually with diplomas from the same institutions. Some of us coming from what might be called, with a nod to Hillary Clinton, the academic plantation, are only too well aware of the lengths to which our university taskmasters now go in order to compel diversity.

Four Heads and First Principles

Each head of the conservative coalition favors its own first principle or foundational concept, which serves as the standard by which it judges what is right or good. For the traditionalist, that concept is History or Culture, meaning the heritage that has come down to us and that is our own. Count it our great fortune, too, that this Culture happens to be good. In a recent book by Samuel Huntington titled *Who are We?* which has been much lauded by traditionalists, the author proceeds to trace the core of America's identity to its original culture, in existence long before the Revolution in the practices and beliefs of our New England settlers.[1] He labels this culture "Anglo-Protestantism," and it is similar to what Tocqueville refers to as America's "point of departure." Here it is that we should look to find our moorings. Traditionalists today are defenders of the culture—in the case of some of them, gently and urbanely, armed only with their bow ties; in the case of others, more ferociously, menacing anyone who might disturb it. The traditionalists' defense of culture, which on examination turns out to be a remarkably vague and inclusive idea, is less important to them for what it affirms than for what it opposes. Traditionalists mistrust all efforts at full-scale rational structuring in politics, deploring the introduction of theory or general ideas. They even have reservations, for example, about the opening paragraph of the Declaration of Independence, with its talk about Nature and Nature's law. Such abstract thinking leads inevitably to errors and excesses. Culture is good in large part because no one ever had to think it up or devise it. It is just there, having evolved in a specific place or context. Traditionalists prefer what grows in politics—hence "culture," originally an agricultural term—to what is made.

For the neoconservative today, the foundational concept is natural right, which is a fancy or theoretical way of saying that the standard of right or good, so far as political or social action is concerned, is thought to be ascertainable by human reason. An idea of right derived from reason would apply in principle to all, or would be universally valid, however much distinct cultural influences might impede its recognition or make impracticable its acceptance. It follows as well for the neoconservative that human thought or reason, though vastly constrained by circumstances, can be an instrument to help alter or structure the environment in which we live. For neoconservatives, the American Founding is an emblematic event because of its wholesale framing of a system by "reflection and choice"; for traditionalists, the Founding is better viewed as a piece of evolution in the development of Anglo-Protestant cultural values.

Where prudence for the traditionalist is equated with caution or defensiveness, for the neoconservative it can sometimes mean boldness. Neoconservatives, in line with traditionalists, concede that most of what has been offered politically under the name of reason in recent times—say the last couple of centuries or so—has been dangerous abstraction and ideology; they hold, nevertheless, that the course of correction must come ultimately from reason itself, not from its renunciation, which leads to severe excesses of its own. It will not do to throw the baby out with the bathwater.

For the libertarian, the foundational concept is "spontaneous order," a postulate that holds that a tendency is operative in human affairs for things to work out for themselves and to cohere, provided no effort is made by an outside force to interfere by seeking to impose an overall order. The only order that is good is one that is set up to ensure the free play of spontaneous processes, or a "system of natural liberty."[2] Liberty, which the libertarian values for its own sake, is perhaps most important because it helps assure spontaneous order by foiling government planning. Most of us are familiar with the idea of spontaneous order from the study of economics, where it goes under an assumed name of "the invisible hand." The invisible hand works behind our backs to ensure that while each person or unit pursues its own particular interest unconcerned with the whole, the result will be to the benefit of all. For libertarians, economics, far from being a dismal science, is queen of the sciences and architectonic for all other forms of knowledge. Most libertarians would prefer to spend their time breathing the rarefied atmosphere of pure economic speculation, but, duty calling, some have descended to lower realms, applying economic principles to social policy, cultural policy, and even international relations.

For those in the Religious Right, the foundational concept is biblical faith. In contrast to the other foundational concepts, faith is not concerned in the first instance with politics, but with another realm altogether: our relation to the transcendent. It is therefore not surprising that many who took their bearings from faith were for much of the last century apolitical, or at any rate they never thought it correct to organize collectively on the basis of a concern emanating from faith. Involvement in politics on grounds relating to faith was therefore sporadic and arose on specific issues. But about thirty years ago or so, in response to an assessment of a new situation characterized by a growing political and cultural threat to faith, a conviction grew that the two realms—the political-cultural and the religious—intersect, not just sporadically on particular issues, but on an ongoing, systematic basis. Some people of faith therefore chose self-consciously to organize and engage more directly in political and cultural affairs. This decision was the basis of what became known by the 1980s as the Religious Right.

Faith as a foundational concept in the political realm does not aim to supply a complete standard of political right. It supports a second-order political-cultural project related to the interests or concerns of faith. Stated defensively, that project includes collective action designed to create and protect havens conducive to fostering life committed to faith. In practice, this has meant undertaking efforts to counterbalance forces working in politics and culture that are indifferent or hostile to faith. But the project is misunderstood if only its defensive aspect is considered. There is a positive element as well. Recall here the older idea, one originally of Puritan roots, of America's role as an instrument in the service of the transcendent. As one minister, speaking at almost the same time as the issuance of the Declaration of Independence, reminded Americans: "The providences of God in first planting his church in this, then howling wilderness, and in delivering and preserving it to this day . . . are reckoned among the most glorious events that are to be found in history, in these later ages of the world. And there are yet more glorious events in the womb of providence."[3]

For those of faith, the adoption of the legal Constitution in no way abrogated this understanding. America may have been assigned a special place in serving a higher cause. For many of the faithful, it has always been thought that there is a second and unwritten constitution that is meant to operate alongside the legal one. Because these two constitutions deal with largely distinct matters, there was no need to combine them into a single document—indeed, it would be harmful to the purposes of both realms ever to attempt to do so. The two constitutions existed together in the hearts and thoughts of many Americans and were complementary in practice. For those of this view, America is not fully America—and cannot be fully loved and cherished—if this unwritten constitution is renounced and if faith then survives here, at best, as merely one belief among many. Would it be too strong to say that an America without faith is "unconstitutional"?

One of the major activities occurring within the Religious Right today is the reformulation of this project in a form that speaks to our times. Conditions have changed, and the specific character of the positive project must change as well. Once conceived as a mission of the "reformed" church only, it is today being reconceived—I am not speaking of the fine points of theology—as a common enterprise among those devoted to biblical faith to cope with a culture that conceives itself as "postreligious."

The Objections of Four Heads to Liberalism

These four foundational concepts—culture, natural right, spontaneous order, and faith—supply the basis for much of what conservatives find

25

objectionable in liberalism. There is agreement among conservatives on many of these objections, but each part of the movement, on the basis of its foundational concept, has assumed a special role in criticizing a different facet of liberalism. For the traditionalist, liberalism's most repulsive feature is a casual progressivism that disdains our heritage. Liberals shop for the new, the trendy and (metaphorically speaking) the "European" against the traditional and the American. Liberals are by preference cosmopolitan, "transnational," or multicultural; they are more anxious to assume someone else's perspective than our own. The posture is diametrically opposed to the traditionalist's view, which is proud of our own culture—in part just because it is our own.

Neoconservatives object to liberalism's relativism, its claim that human thought leads to the conclusion that there is no standard of right. Liberals may know what is right by following the dictates of the heart—they speak constantly of humanitarianism and universal compassion—and they sometimes seek, without coherence, to derive from relativism itself an absolute standard of tolerance. But when it comes to the test, they back away from proclaiming any grounds for a rational standard of right. For liberalism, the promulgation of such a standard smacks of arrogance and intolerance, leading to excesses and extremism. Leading liberal intellectuals favor the theoretical position known as "anti-foundationalism," which holds that advanced democracies are truest to their calling when they foreswear a foundational concept of any kind, political or religious. To neoconservatives, relativism is the antithesis of natural right; it has translated into a fecklessness in pursuing the national purpose, which was on display during the Cold War and is on display today in the War on Terror.

For the libertarian, liberalism is objectionable because of its reflexive preference for regulation and planning. Liberalism is virtually synonymous with big government. No efforts to swear off this addiction—including solemn pronouncements that the era of big government is over—can succeed. Liberalism is a repeat offender and perennial antagonist to the "system of natural liberty."

The Religious Right objects to liberalism's secularism. Secularism goes well beyond the espousal of an interpretation of the Constitution, where it has sought to erect a famous "wall of separation" between religion and the state. Its fundamental objective extends far beyond the legal realm. Liberal secularism is a project in its own right that is bent on eliminating any recognized place for biblical faith as the guiding light of the culture. It will not rest content until faith withdraws from playing any public role, direct or indirect. The conflict of secularism and faith is at the heart of the so-called "culture war."

Analysis of the foundational concepts of the different parts of the conservative movement holds the key to understanding not only their objections to liberalism, but also their criticisms of each other. The two lines of argument are often identical, as conservatives accuse others within the movement of being liberal in all but name. To illustrate this point would take another essay and might be too painful a subject on which to embark. Suffice it to say that the jousting for position within the conservative coalition leads to distortions and misconceptions that threaten the well-being of the movement as a whole.

The Future of Four Heads and One Heart

This volume is intended not just to survey the current state of conservatism, but to ponder its future. I will not hazard speaking of the future in the usual sense of offering prognostications of what will happen. This kind of exercise comes dangerously close to prophesying, and I am only too aware of the dire penalties that attach to false prophecy. Besides, there are more than enough professionals in false prophesying, known as political pundits, and unlike university professors they are paid very handsomely to assume this kind of risk.

Instead, the future I would like briefly to consider is the shape that conservatism should assume if it is to continue its task of leading the nation. In an excess of pride, or perhaps complacency, many conservatives contend that conservatism is the only force capable of offering leadership in America today, because liberalism for the moment is utterly without a positive program. This assessment may be technically correct. But it does not follow that Americans will embrace the leadership option proposed to them. They might just as readily choose to reject it and to tread water. Even among conservatives who tout conservatism's leadership prowess, there are many to be found in this last camp.

Conservatism is not automatically an active force. Indeed, the word conservative itself can connote the very opposite, suggesting a disposition to be hesitant, to go slow, and to wait upon others to lead. Conservatism can remain a dynamic force only if its four heads are ordered in a certain arrangement. That arrangement must place the proponents of natural right and of faith in the initiating roles. They alone possess major projects that speak to the great political issues of our time. Traditionalism is proudly without a positive project and finds its voice in the critical assessment of others' initiatives; it functions best as the "conscience of conservatism." Libertarianism has its focus not on high politics, but on "administration." Failure to master the challenges of administration, which includes such vital matters as managing our budgets and coping with the massive future economic pressures of pensions and medical care, would surely spell the doom of any movement. Yet important as these issues are, they do not constitute the central questions of politics that move the mass of Americans and that define our times. These questions are found in the battle to save civilization from a new barbarism and in the effort within the part of civilization we call the West to sustain a culture of biblical faith. America's role in affecting the outcome on both of these questions is central. As civilization's most important power, it is America's responsibility to craft the basic strategy for thwarting the new barbarism and for carrying the burden of putting that strategy into effect. As the only nation in the West with a large movement to sustain faith, the task seems to have fallen to this nation to keep a lamp burning until a tide is turned.

If a partnership in leadership between neoconservatives and the Religious Right is to succeed, each part needs to be conscious of its role and of the character of its partner. It is here, above all, that avoiding misconceptions is crucial, for there are many who, either from ignorance or a will to deceive, advance arguments that would set these two groups at odds. A major contention is that the foundational concept of natural right is hostile to faith. Its emphasis on reason and natural rights, applying universally to all, is offered somehow as proof; there is nothing special about faith. This position is in error. Properly understood, the American conception of natural law assigns to the political power the solemn charge of protecting rights. But it does not demand the abandonment of a larger or higher purpose. The respect and enforcement of rights is a floor for political life, not a ceiling. Projects that are compatible with respecting these natural rights are not banned from the life of the political community. Natural right on its own does not require the cultivation of biblical faith in the name of the common good, but it is clear that many of its adherents have today become convinced that the project of faith now works largely to that end. Proof of this support is seen in how neoconservatives have teamed with members of the Religious Right to work together on key issues such as the composition of the courts, genetic engineering, and school choice.

If proponents of natural right have found much that is compatible in the project of faith, the reverse is also the case. For one thing, it has been sheer calumny on the part of liberals and secularists to suggest that proponents of faith are somehow hostile to the protection of natural rights and therefore at odds with neoconservatives (and everyone else). The Religious Right has pursued its aims on top of the system of natural rights, which it fully supports, not in opposition to it. The more important point that bears on a partnership is the partial agenda of the Religious Right. The project of faith is concerned with a limited mission, not directly with managing the whole of a political agenda. For its own sake, it may never want to be more than a powerful influence that works within a coalition, rather than a force that claims full responsibility for exercising rule. It therefore needs a partner in governing. It would be foolish, of course, to think that the different priorities of these two parts of the coalition will not sometimes conflict. They will. Nevertheless, on a realistic and successful management of these divergences hinges the real future of the conservative movement.

3

The Irony of Conservative Success

George W. Carey

A SURVEY OF THE present American political scene provides, I believe, the background and point of departure for examining more permanent and basic aspects of American institutions and politics that pose enormous obstacles to the realization of principles long associated with traditional conservatism. More specifically, the eclipse (some might say the disappearance) of traditional conservatism when both Congress and the presidency are controlled by Republicans is no anomaly; it is, instead, the predictable outgrowth of an interplay between the political culture and institutions. Let me begin with three salient observations relating to conservatism and to our present political environment.

Conservatism Rightly Understood

First, a consensus exists among media pundits, editorial writers, and the like— and, therefore, one would assume among wide sectors of the politically aware as well—that the current Bush administration is among the most conservative in history. Some media commentators, perhaps most, even regard it as the most conservative ever. In any event, there is no dearth of analyses that stress President George W. Bush's conservative values and outlook, as well as how they find expression in the policies he advances. Moreover, liberal Democrats who take exception with administration policies contribute to this consensus by frequently characterizing these policies as conservative in the extreme. In a more general vein, it is not at all uncommon to hear that, with the election of Bush, and with Republican congressional majorities throughout most of his tenure, the country has witnessed a triumph of conservative principles over the badly divided, defensive, and intellectually barren forces of liberalism.[1]

Second, what is not widely known, save in certain "conservative" circles, is that there are those—including once avid readers of *National Review*, diehard Reagan supporters, long-time subscribers to avowedly conservative causes, and the like—who regard Bush as something other than conservative.[2] Indeed, what many call, for lack of a better term, "paleo-" or "traditional conservatives" see the Bush administration as actually advancing the cause of liberalism or, if not that, as pursuing the path of a calculated, poll-driven political expediency devoid of any principle. Consequently, in their view, to apply the word *conservative* to Bush and his administration, as the media routinely does, not only is misleading but also debases conservatism. In short, there is now an apparently unbridgeable divide between traditional conservatives and the Bush administration on major policy matters.

There are aspects of this chasm that bear mention. It can be viewed as the fruition of bitter conflicts between neoconservatives and "paleo-" or "traditional" conservatives over policies and personalities that first arose early in the Reagan administration and that have simmered ever since. From the perspective of the traditionalists, the media's failure to note this conflict, as well as its penchant for conflating neoconservatism with the broader, older ("traditional") conservatism, has contributed to a distorted and truncated understanding of conservatism particularly among large, politically unsophisticated sectors of the American people. Of course, what may well account for the media's skewed perception of conservatism is the ascendancy of the neoconservatives to positions of prominence in the Bush administration and in the major think tanks; that is, they simply overshadow the traditionalists in the political arena, and are, therefore, more readily accessible to the media. But whatever the reason, this conflation has led some traditional conservatives to abandon the very term *conservative*, arguing either that it no longer has meaning (certainly not that which it possessed prior to Bush's first election) or that the very use of the term leads to a misunderstanding or confusion too troublesome to unravel.[3]

Third, the Bush II administration has also drastically altered the character of the Republican Party, moving it away from its longstanding conservative positions. This much seems obvious when the Democrats can boast, and not without substantial justification, of being the party of fiscal responsibility. Congressional Republicans, following the lead of the administration, now seem unconcerned about expansive and expensive long-term federal programs, centralization, the growth of bureaucracy, a growing debt, or balanced budgets. Or, again acceding to the administration's wishes, they seem to have watered down or abandoned positions on significant policy issues, e.g., farm subsidies, the role of the Department of Education, and school vouchers.

To be sure, not all of the administration's policies are displeasing to the more traditional conservatives, the most notable exceptions being perhaps taxation policy, most judicial appointments, and positions on certain cultural issues.[4] The fact remains, nevertheless, that there have been highly significant deviations from basic principles long shared by both the Republican Party and the traditional conservatives. To see this clearly, let us suppose that at some point during William Jefferson Clinton's second term a prominent politician had advanced the policies now embraced by the Bush administration? How would his political outlook have been characterized?

But, if there be any doubts about deviations from traditional conservatism and the Republican heritage in the domestic field, there can be none over the major goals and principles of Bush II's foreign policy. His aggressive foreign policy, perhaps best described as Wilsonianism on steroids, has its roots in the traditions of the Democratic Party and clearly runs counter to well-established conservative principles. The Iraq War and the reasons given to support it, for example, would hardly find support in the writings of the more traditional conservatives such as Russell Kirk, Robert Nisbet, or Richard M. Weaver.[5]

Most interesting in this connection are Condoleezza Rice's remarks at the *Institut d'Etudes Politiques de Paris* (February 8, 2005) that reveal a mindset totally at odds with the intellectual foundations of traditional conservatism. After pointing out how the histories of the United States and France are "intertwined" (the 1989 "bicentennial celebration of the French Revolution and the Rights of Man" was also "the two-hundreth anniversary of our nation's Constitution and our Bill of Rights"), [6] she adds that these "shared celebrations" were something more "than mere coincidence." On the contrary, as she would have it, "The founders of both the French and American republics were inspired by the very same values, and by each other. They shared the universal values of freedom and democracy and human dignity that have inspired men and women across the globe for centuries."[7]

Traditional conservatives, of course, can only look upon these remarks as rank heresy because they contradict the teachings of Edmund Burke— regarded by many scholars to be the "father" of modern conservatism— and the philosophical heritage which they inspired. Her remarks, whether intended or not, link American foreign policy to those very principles against which Burke and a long line of conservative thinkers have inveighed.[8] The traditionalist, thus, is to be forgiven his bewilderment and even resentment when he confronts statements of this kind from the leading international spokesman for an administration reputed by many to be the most conservative in our nation's history.

What the foregoing shows is that in a very short period of time a major transformation in the American political landscape has occurred. The Republican Party has, so to speak, changed its spots virtually without attracting much critical attention, the major exception being the objections of disillusioned and disgruntled traditionalists. Moreover, along with the transformation of the Republican Party, we have witnessed a corresponding transformation of the popularly accepted understanding of conservatism. The two, this is to say, go hand in hand, with neoconservatism providing a "cover" that allowed the administration to drastically transform the character of the Republican Party without its spokesmen being obliged to renounce conservatism. All this was facilitated because, with a few exceptions, neither the Democrats nor the media were either interested in or aware of philosophical divisions within Republican ranks.[9]

Conservatism's Permanent Concerns

Assuming that I am essentially correct in describing the salient aspects of the transformation of the Republican Party, wherein do we find the more basic and permanent concerns to which I referred at the outset? We come to see the nature of these concerns by inquiring first into how Bush II could accomplish what he has in such short order without any apparent "rebellion" by a significant number of his own party in Congress. After all, it would seem that a transformation of the dimensions alluded to above would involve far greater intraparty conflict and dissent than we have witnessed. Instead we find the rebellion, if it can be called that, confined to a small number of Representatives. The question thus becomes, Why have Republicans in Congress been so compliant?

To a great degree the reasons for this compliance are attributable to the nature of our political culture and institutions. To begin with, the president nowadays has abundant means at his disposal to bring recalcitrant congressional members of his party around to his views. Republicans in Congress, for instance, are no doubt thankful to Bush II for his generosity in allowing record expenditures for "pork barrel" projects. But, more significantly, the presidency, being the only elective national office, is the main prize sought in the struggle between the two major parties. And there are very substantial reasons why it is valued so highly. The powers of the office have grown enormously over time so that the rewards, honors and favors that flow from controlling it provide strong incentives for members of Congress to defend and to support a president of their own party. They want to share in this bounty, which is also important to their own political success, and they are smart enough to know that, if members of the congressional wing of the party split with their president, intraparty conflicts might well result that could imperil continued control of the presidency. Thus, any sizeable congressional group, even one united on doctrines or policy, being fully aware of just how high the costs can potentially be in defying a president of their party, is most reluctant to do so save in the most extreme cases.

Fifty years ago James Burnham lamented that Congress, once the dominant institution in our constitutional system, had been eclipsed by the presidency.[10] Yet, there is good reason to believe that in the intervening decades, despite Nixon's resignation and Clinton's impeachment, the presidency has grown stronger relative to Congress and, as evidenced by the behavior of the Bush II administration, has done so in significant, nonconstitutional ways. Woodrow Wilson's observations provide here a framework for understanding the nature of these new dimensions of presidential power. He was among the first to set forth the outlines of a presidentially oriented system that in many respects is a forerunner of the disciplined and responsible party schemes so attractive to many modern American political scientists.

Given the diffusive constitutional distribution of authority, Wilson saw the need for strong political parties in order to assure accountability, responsibility, and reasoned policies. In this vein, he viewed the political party, much as moderns do, as a mechanism that could overcome the undesirable separation between Congress, the lawmaking institution, and the executive, the executor of the law. He prophesied that the president's role would grow immensely: as the demands of the office increased over time "incumbents . . . will more and more come to feel that they are administering it in its truest purpose and with the greatest effect by regarding themselves as less and less executive officers and more and more directors of affairs and leaders of the nation,—men of counsel and of the sort of action that makes for enlightenment."[11]

Wilson's prediction concerning presidential leadership has come to pass. What also seems to have transpired, as we see from Bush's rejection of traditional Republican/conservative principles, is that the president is now the head of his political party, representing not what Wilson's intellectual disciples would prefer, i.e., a leader who ably presents and advances the policies and the principles that are at least shared by the "grassroots" of the party,[12] but instead, a leader who is free within the bounds of political reality to redefine what the party stands for, even if this means changing the direction of the party by repudiating or abandoning its traditional principles and values. For reasons I have set forth, the modern president in this capacity will carry the party with him, provided he does not take outlandish positions that would endanger the party's status or adversely affect his party's congressional delegation. Yet, as Bush II's example attests, even with these and similar limitations, the president still has a wide latitude in determining the party's direction.[13] This is particularly true in the foreign policy area where, normally, there are even fewer restrictions on the president's course of action.

The question arises, is this development good or bad? For instance, the country might well benefit from a periodic reorientation of the political parties brought about by presidential dictation. Or it might be that the common good is promoted when presidents are free to shed their partisanship and promote policies and principles more in keeping with the public interest. As I have indicated, however, neither of these outcomes seems likely given the character of our political culture. Beyond this, there is ample reason to believe that presidential "leadership" of this kind does not bode well from the perspective of traditional conservatives. Why so? The answer comes from recognizing the simple fact that Progressives have long dreamed of a presidentially oriented constitutional order, one in which the president dominates the Congress. The periodic polls which consistently reveal that historians and political scientists, most of them confirmed liberals, give their highest rankings to "strong" presidents—i.e., those who have asserted and expanded the prerogatives of the presidency—simply manifest this view. Generations of Americans have been weaned on the notion that strong presidents are also "great" presidents. What is more, as Burnham documents, and what is still the case today, in American history and politics texts and commentaries, the presidency is normally pictured in the most positive terms, particularly in contrast to Congress. Again, Woodrow Wilson set the tone in describing the president as "representative of no constituency, but of the whole people"; "the political leader of the nation"; "the only voice in national affairs."[14] And this vision has been reinforced by normally sober historians and political scientists who see the president as the one individual best equipped to express the "general will" of the nation.[15]

Progressives are quite correct in assuming that their values are best served by strong presidents, but for a reason that is not sufficiently emphasized, namely, the presidency is an office inherently suited to their goals and aspirations. As a constitutional office, of course, it is well structured to satisfy their normal penchant for centralization—in this context, centralized decision-making without what they deem to be the undue, perhaps corrupting, influence of parochial or local interests. But other, more intangible factors, relating to the status of the office and the character of the individuals who aspire to it, influence the substance and the tenor of these decisions.

Consider, to begin with, that presidential aspirants are pathological, even though their pathology may not as yet be clinically defined. The distant prospects of fame and power must be sufficient to overcome the trials and tribulations of campaigning for and holding office. For instance, to say nothing of the physical demands and pressures, they must anticipate that their lives and those of their family will be scrutinized in great detail; that rumors and falsehoods about them and their family will abound; that their positions will be distorted; or that, in the course of their campaigns and tenure in office, they must be prepared to fudge the truth and even lie. Only extremely ambitious individuals with oversized, fortified egos, at least sufficiently so to mitigate or make bearable these and a host of other deprivations and debasements, can hope to win the office. It is hardly surprising, then, when we learn that once in office (or maybe even before election) individuals with such steely egoism and overwhelming ambition start to think about how they will be viewed by historians of the future or, what amounts to much the same thing, what their "legacy" will be.

We can profitably ask, how would an incumbent president go about securing a favorable judgment down the line? If the past is our guide—and it might well be our most reliable guide—he should try to be a "strong" president in the sense I have indicated. We already have a clue about what this entails: namely, expanding the prerogatives and powers of the presidency.[16] But there is more than this involved. Indeed, the expansion of powers and prerogatives by themselves scarcely seems sufficient unless they are associated with bold action, leadership in crisis, or policies directed toward eliminating or resolving perennial problems or concerns. As frequently remarked, events and circumstances beyond the control of presidents—e.g., wars, depression— dictate their place in history. That is, when they seem to rise to the occasion, to meet the challenges posed by impersonal "forces" and events, they have been accorded high status.

What, however, of incumbents who do not have the opportunity to face such challenges? Lacking war, economic collapse, or some widespread catastrophe, how can they secure a high place in history? One obvious answer is to pursue policies, preferably new and bold policies, that will be looked upon with great favor by those who are to judge in the future. Again, while there is no way of knowing for sure what policies will serve this purpose, the past helps to provide a guide. Incumbents who have expanded the role and the functions of the national government, who have promoted greater political centralization, who have initiated programs designed to promote security along with greater economic and social equality—those who, in sum, have advanced the progressive agenda—are assured perhaps not the highest status, but a thoroughly respectable one. To put this otherwise, the incumbent concerned about posterity's view of his legacy has to think about what standards or criteria will be used for judging it. And, in this respect, a sense that the continued ascendance of progressive values is inevitable seems to prevail. At the very least, incumbents know that the pursuit of a progressive agenda is likely to compensate for their failures and shortcomings in other areas.

Conservatism and the Separation of Powers

What I have advanced thus far are two interrelated propositions. First, the powers and the status of modern presidents allow them great leeway in transforming or even abandoning party principles, especially when an incumbent's party controls both chambers of Congress. Indeed, under these circumstances, a president may even alter the party's course by unilaterally promulgating new goals and principles. Second, in transforming the old or in setting forth the new, presidents are strongly inclined to move in directions that advance progressive values and goals. It is in these terms that the transformation of the Republican Party by the Bush II administration and its embrace of progressive values is best understood. Though beyond the scope of our concern here, I also believe that this inclination accounts for the "leftward" drift of the Republican Party since World War II.[17] If this analysis is largely correct, this drift can be expected to continue into the indefinite future.

These more or less political concerns are closely related to others which are more theoretical and relate to the whys and wherefores of our constitutional structures. To appreciate these concerns fully in the context with which we are concerned, some background is necessary. I can best start by noting that political parties, as the progressive reform literature emphasizes, provide the means for overcoming the separation of powers. The arguments against the separation of powers advanced by progressives reveal a hostility toward the constitutional fragmentation of powers; from the progressive vantage point this fragmentation makes the passage of coherent and necessary policy extremely difficult and blurs the lines of responsibility and accountability. Parties provide the link or thread between institutions; they are the instrumentalities that can overcome the constitutionally mandated fragmentation, thereby enabling the branches (principally Congress and the presidency) to act in unison.

On the other hand, it is apparent that our Founding Fathers viewed the separation of powers from an almost entirely different perspective. A separation of the legislative, executive, and judicial branches was felt to be essential across the entire political spectrum. In fact, Madison in *Federalist* essay no. 47 feels obliged to respond to those Anti-Federalists who were contending that the proposed Constitution blended these powers to a dangerous degree. In this same essay, Madison expresses a view that was widely shared; namely, the very concentration of these three functions in the hands of the one, the few, or the many was tyranny. It was, it should be remarked, the mere concentration of powers, quite apart from the purposes for which they were employed, that constituted tyranny. As the *Federalist* text makes clear, concerns over maintaining the separation of powers and ensuring that each branch possess a will of its own are intimately linked to securing the rule of law, to preventing arbitrary and capricious rule. As such, the principle of separation, involving both powers and functions, was considered essential to the preservation of liberty and, we may infer, it was also felt to be a prerequisite for stable republican government.

From the vantage point of those who share the framers' concerns about the concentration of powers, the potential dangers inherent in the president's role as party leader are evident, particularly when his party controls both the Senate and the House. Abuses can take the form of discriminatory legislation, not perhaps in the sense or to the degree the framers had in mind, but rather as carefully crafted measures intended to secure the party's popular base for the long term. This, of course, entails the use of the machinery of government and its resources for maximum partisan advantage to the fullest extent possible without encountering an opposition that might diminish the party's popular support. But this strategy is hardly surprising. The most casual observer of American politics soon realizes that the goal of gaining and retaining power— that which, we should recall, accounts for the abrupt transformation of political parties—is paramount. Control of the legislative and executive branches helps to attain a clear unimpeded path to this end.

What should not be overlooked when a party possesses control—particularly with the growth of the administrative state—is the relative freedom that the president and his administration enjoy, since neither legislative branch is likely to undertake serious investigations of their activities and policies lest it embarrass the party. In short, when a single party dominates, there are no "makeweights" (to use Bertrand de Jouvenel's terminology),[18] save as an issue that might make its way into the judicial system. The president is a single, strong-willed individual who, with the example of his most admired predecessors before him (i.e., the "strong" presidents), is bound to feel the need to preserve and to advance the institutional interests of his office. In this regard, neither chamber of Congress is his match; circumstances dictate that he is bound to feel the pull of institutional interest far more intensely than members of a numerous representative assembly, either collectively or individually. For this reason, a president, far more than Congress, is inclined to "push the envelope" in striving to expand his powers and to do so with anticipation of success.

Now it is true, as I have already intimated, that one-party control of the legislative and the executive functions has not resulted in tyranny in the "hard" sense. Moreover, the country is wealthy enough so that whatever discrimination is suffered by one faction can be, and usually is, mitigated sometime down the line according to its preferential treatment. Certainly, the fact that we have a competitive two-party system also helps to restrain excesses by the temporarily dominant party. These mitigating factors, however, have not proven sufficient to prevent a party, when in total control of the legislative process, from initiating sweeping and costly social programs of one sort or another that have proven ineffective and wasteful.

The party's quest to secure continued dominance by catering to large sectors of the population and the president's desire for a "legacy," joined with the realization that the window of opportunity might close, are conducive to such extravagant and ill-considered policies. These and similar policies also reflect a mindset that seems to predominate among the politically active in both parties, namely, that government is omnipotent, that the ills that plague society and individuals can be cured through legislation. The result is that the reach of the government expands to embrace more and more activities, functions, and problems, an expansion that increases when one party comes to control the entire policymaking apparatus.

The lack of makeweights also imperils the constitutional limitations and restraints on the range of the government's authority and functions that are central to traditional conservatism. In their absence, state and local autonomy and the principle of federalism are respected only to the degree that they do not interfere with realization of the president's "legacy" or the pursuit of policies designed to secure and to expand the party's base. With the initiation of new programs and expansion of the old comes a corresponding increase in the scope of the national government's authority, normally with greater controls over all other levels of government and private sectors as well. And given a compliant Congress, power also centralizes in the presidency, thereby compromising the separation of powers. In this process, conservative values and principles are repudiated. In fact, though, what we witness is perhaps far graver: A base politics virtually devoid of principles.

Lastly, the president's traditional role in setting our foreign policy, coupled with his authority as commander-in-chief of our armed forces, has allowed him to commit the nation to prolonged hostilities, whether by seeking a declaration of war or through other means. That the president can lead the nation into war, leaving Congress with essentially no alternative but to give its assent after the fact, is recognized in many quarters as a problem that begs solution.[19] It must be acknowledged that presidents will unilaterally lead the country into war even when there is a "divided" or "split" government, that is when the opposition party controls one or both chambers of Congress. What is to be noted, however, is that the president and his policies are at least challenged and brought to public attention when there is such a divided government, sometimes with great effect.[20]

There would appear to be, therefore, less possibility of a president unscrupulously endeavoring to secure his legacy through war—that is, becoming a "war president" by instigating an unnecessary war or pursuing policies designed to provoke hostilities—when there is an effective makeweight.

Conservatism and Countervailing Forces

The arguments presented here clearly point toward the virtues of a government in which the parties share effective power; a government in which there is an effective counterweight to the president. Many commentators have maintained that most Americans, although they may not be able to articulate the reasons why, also favor power-sharing. Their instincts are, I believe, fundamentally sound, for the reasons I have set forth. Certainly the arguments for partisan power-sharing deserve more public exposure than they have been accorded, the more so in light of the consequences that seem to flow inevitably from one-party control.

At another level, what I have argued provides the stipulations necessary for answering a question that has perplexed traditional conservatives over the years, namely, which institution—the presidency or Congress—is more deserving of their support over the long haul? Which institution is the more inherently conservative? To the extent that the foregoing analysis is correct, the answer would be: Congress more than the presidency, but only when party differences enable it to exercise a truly independent will, to demonstrate some institutional pride and backbone along the lines that the framers envisioned.[21]

Finally, and what is central to my concern, one cannot help but marvel at how easily a modern president can utterly transform the character of his political party—its goals and what it stands for. In this process, we see that principle is abandoned or rationalized into meaninglessness when it stands athwart the overriding interest of the political party to gain and perpetuate its control of presidential powers. For this reason, principles, even those relating to concerns about the long-term common good, can never have deep roots in the American political culture: the quest for control of the enormous powers of the presidency dictates that parties will assume positions calculated to achieve victory. There is nothing new in this. What is new, as I have tried to show, is that a major factor for a party in this calculation, particularly when it controls Congress, is the imperative to support its incumbent president, including his ambitions to secure a "legacy." None of this bodes well for either principled parties or politics. Ultimately, one lesson for traditional conservatives, who more than most see the need for a politics guided and restrained by enduring principles, seems clear enough: They should never swear undying allegiance to any political party.

4

A Plea for Constitutional Conservatism

Harvey C. Mansfield

CONSTITUTIONAL CONSERVATISM IS A blend of populism and elitism, a good thing made of two dubious ingredients. To explain what that is in brief compass, I will begin from the *dilemma* of conservatism, move to the *task* of conservatism—which I believe to be defending liberalism in the wide sense—and, last, come to the *form* of conservatism in the American Constitution.

The Dilemma of Conservatism

What is conservatism? Conservatism is a correlate of liberalism; it follows upon liberalism; it is liberalism's little brother. "Conservatism" began to be heard as a political term only after the French Revolution when it was provoked by the manifest excesses of the Revolution into opposition. But what kind of opposition? Was conservatism to be the alternative to liberal revolution or was it to supply the defects of that revolution so as to make it work? And there were opponents of the Revolution, usually called reactionaries but still conservatives, who wanted to return to the old regime and therefore supported monarchy and religion, the throne and the altar. But there were also conservative liberals such as Benjamin Constant, François Guizot, and Alexis de Tocqueville who accepted the Revolution while blaming its excesses. Later, the great liberal John Stuart Mill described the party of progress and the party of order as correlates of a liberal regime, the one making advances, the other providing digestion.

Here, at the origin of conservatism, we see its fundamental dilemma: Is it the alternative to liberalism or does it make liberalism work better than it would on its own? We can put this in fewer words: Does conservatism *go back* or does it *go slow*? It is a dilemma because these are opposite strategies that require opposite behavior. If conservatism is the alternative to liberalism, it needs principles and goes back in history to find them. Going back is a revolution against the present, against the liberal status quo; it is a counterrevolution. It brings turmoil, upset, and accusations of "extremism." Think of the so-called Republican Revolution of 1994. Its maker, Newt Gingrich, accused the previous Republican leadership in Congress of being the "tax collector for the Welfare State," that is, too willing to raise money for projects Republicans ought to oppose on principle. In return, he was labeled an extremist like the fervent extremists on the left.

If on the other hand conservatism supplies the defects of liberalism and goes slow, it must forget principles and accommodate with liberalism. Conservatives of this sort may be called "responsible," like George H. W. Bush and Robert Dole, and they are responsible because they take charge of a situation they do not care for but make the best of. For such conservatives all ideas cause problems, including conservative ideas. The elder Bush spoke deprecatingly of the "vision thing," which he was alleged to lack. (This was his wonderful contribution to our political vocabulary.) Visions are bad; they are closer to nightmares than sweet dreams, but in either case they are dreams. In a democracy "vision" almost always means the vision of a more perfect democracy, of what we already have. It's imaginary because perfect democracy is impossible, and it's not very imaginative because, as we know from Tocqueville, the dominant passion in America is toward ever more democracy.

The greatest conservative thinker is undoubtedly Edmund Burke (though he lived before the name "conservative" was coined and he called himself a Whig). In Burke too we find a tension between principle and prudence. Burke relies on natural law, on principles taught us spontaneously (by nature) and through reflection (according to nature) that guide our lives. These principles go back in time to "sound antiquity" (Burke's phrase), to medieval scholasticism, and to seventeenth- and eighteenth-century thinkers of natural public law. Yet Burke's version of natural law is quite special to him because it is designed to avoid causing social disruption, to say nothing of revolution. For Burke a "great, fundamental part" of natural law is prescription, a concept taken from Roman law (positive law, not natural; and private law, not public) that allows one to gain possession of property after long, uncontested use of it, and to lose it after a similar failure to exercise one's possession. This is Burke's peculiar contribution to the theory of natural law, a natural law favorable to practice rather than theory.

Burke, moreover, opposed the French Revolution—which claimed to be based on natural right—by contrasting it to the English Revolution of 1688. The makers of the English Revolution, he said, took pains to avoid stating any principle such as that government must recognize the people's right of consent, and they justified overturning the Stuart kings only because it was strictly necessary in these circumstances for maintaining the liberty of the people. Thus the English Revolution was a mere adjustment made by prudence, claiming no more definite principle than doing the wise thing when compelled by necessity. This justification amounts to an accommodation to fact rather than an assertion against things as they are, and it is expressly designed to prevent revolution from becoming a precedent for later imitation. In the most eminent conservative thinker as well as in recent American political history we see both principle rising above circumstances and prudence working within the bounds of the status quo.

Conservatism is thus in a dilemma between going back and going slow. Neither strategy is satisfactory by itself; hence both are inevitable. Conservatives cannot consistently be responsible or revolutionary; so perhaps they must be both. Being both is inconsistent, but it might be prudent. Conservatives can try to have it both ways: Using prudence keeps you from being an ideologue, but holding to principle keeps you from being inconsistent and opportunistic.

The Task of Conservatism

With the double strategy of principle and prudence, go back and go slow, conservatives must take on the task of defending liberalism. To defend liberalism is to defend its principles, the best principles of liberalism. But it is also prudent, because liberalism will not go away and if it did, the forces replacing it would be worse—as we see in the Islamic fascists. By defending liberalism I mean of course defending American liberalism from its foreign enemies but also, and primarily, from the errors of those today called "liberals." To do this requires defending liberals in the broader, generic sense of those who profit from and who therefore should defend the whole regime of liberalism. This is hard to do because the original liberalism, which I call generic, has lost its unity and is now divided between liberals in the narrow sense of today's usage and conservatives, between Left and Right.

The leaders of these two parties are intellectuals and businessmen, those who excel in talking or writing and those who know better than most how to make money. John Locke was the founder of liberalism because, being a philosopher above these two groups, he was able to unite them. He did this with an argument for toleration, which appealed to the intellectuals who wanted freedom from the censorship and censoriousness of the church, and with an argument for private property that justified, again against the church, the "heaping up" of money without limit by businessmen. In these two arguments, given political effect in constitutional government, Locke forged an alliance between two sorts of ambitious men who could work in comity if not together. This was the original unity of liberalism that conservatives today, wishing to defend liberalism as a whole, must keep in mind.

The greatest critic of liberalism was not a conservative, not Edmund Burke, but Jean-Jacques Rousseau. It was he who shattered the unity of Locke's liberalism. He attacked Locke's notion of liberty, saying that it was not the liberty of citizens but of bourgeois, of town dwellers who had not fashioned liberty for themselves by their own act but had received it as a gift from the government, the king. Thus the generic liberal came to be labeled a bourgeois, a term used after Rousseau, and still at present, to deride the liberal. ("Middle class" is used in the same way, as in the phrase "middle-class morality," made famous by George Bernard Shaw.) Critics of liberalism following Rousseau attacked it from the right and the left, and they came to be called intellectuals or the intelligentsia (from the Russian). Intellectuals no longer considered themselves to be members of the bourgeoisie (though many of them would be attacked as "bourgeois intellectuals"). In their view they were released from the bourgeoisie by virtue of their criticism of it. Rousseau himself, it may be noted, was a stronger critic of Enlightenment intellectuals than of less pretentious bourgeois moneymakers.

Rousseau saw that liberalism had opposite defects: it was thoroughly selfish because it ignored the community, and it was ignoble because it promoted the mediocre life of commerce. In the nineteenth century the first defect was adopted by the Left in socialism and communism, and the second by the Right in what later came to be fascism and Nazism. Both these movements flourished in the twentieth century before they were defeated. But as long as we have liberalism, both movements will probably return, though perhaps in a different form we will find difficult to recognize, because both answer to essential defects in liberalism.

The postmodern movement today derives from Rousseau, who was the first and best critic of modernity, that is, modern liberalism. He too was "postmodern" in the sense of going beyond modernity without escaping from it, though he did have a coherent political position to offer as the postmoderns today do not. The latter continue Rousseau's critique of the bourgeoisie, and the "culture war" we hear of is between the postmoderns and conservatives (followers of Raymond Aron in France and neoconservatives in America, for example) who defend the bourgeoisie against intellectuals. Nowadays conservatives also defend the *intellect* against the intellectuals, for as a long-term consequence of Rousseau's critique of reason and science (given added power and a peculiar twist by Nietzsche), intellectuals have lost faith in the very rationality that distinguishes them as a class. In America today academic standards have become a political issue: should they be relaxed or upheld? If you are worried about the decline of standards in American education, you are probably a conservative. This new fact is an event of the last half century; there used to be many demanding liberal teachers but now these are rare. By now most liberal teachers have succumbed to the critique coming from antiliberal sources of what used to be called liberal education.

Liberalism, based mostly on self-interest and the virtues of self-interest, is indeed too selfish and ignoble. If liberalism were entirely based on self-interest, it would be, as its critics sometimes say, a mechanism that works of itself because its appeal to self-interest would be unfailing. The intended result would be guaranteed, and liberalism would not need defenders. It would then perhaps be indefensible because it would be thoroughly selfish and ignoble, having no room for the better side of our natures. But in fact liberalism does make an appeal to human nobility that can attract virtuous defenders who are not merely acting on their own self-interest. These defenders must, however, be aware of the complexity of their task; they must be able to look on liberalism as a whole and to some extent from the outside.

So liberalism needs sensible defenders who are aware of its vulnerabilities, who understand its principles and are ready to use prudence in applying them. These sensible defenders are mainly conservatives because most liberals are so devoted to liberal principles that they overlook the weaknesses of those principles. A liberal typically pursues liberal principles regardless of the common good, and a conservative is needed to hold liberalism to the standard of the common good, which includes supporting the virtues of generosity and nobility even though these virtues are not very liberal or easily compatible with self-interest. Liberalism gives freedom to the selfish and the ignoble, and it gives freedom to intemperate critics of selfishness and ignobility. Liberalism will never outgrow its need for prudence. Communism and fascism were defeated in the twentieth century, but they will return, probably in a different form not easily recognized, because human nature not merely follows but also rebels against its own interest. Left and Right will always be with us, and the reason is that they are partly correct in their criticisms of liberalism.

The enemy of conservatism is what is called in America "Big Government," government so large in scope and so beneficent in intent that it tries to save citizens "the trouble of thinking and the pain of living." The quotation is Tocqueville's sarcastic description of the government he called the "Immense Being."[1] Big Government rests on appeal to self-interest and also to motives opposite to self-interest, particularly compassion, even a kind of greatness (President Lyndon Johnson called his version of Big Government "the Great

Society"). Although the phrase "Big Government" is recent, the idea is much older. Tocqueville dates it back ten generations from the French Revolution to the time of Machiavelli, the high point being the statist policy of Cardinals Richelieu and Mazarin in the seventeenth century under Louis XIII and Louis XIV. The French monarchy attempted to apply the idea of rational control to all parts of society, for example, in teaching farmers how to farm better—like the U.S. Department of Agriculture does today.

Rational control is beneficent, not exploitative, mild, not terrifying, and evenhanded, not arbitrary. One could say that it is the idea of modernity itself, the original vision thing. It means the rational control of risk, the risk to one's security. Typically, Tocqueville notes, rational controllers exaggerate their capacity to control risk and end up raising expectations they cannot satisfy, while they remove or destroy the trust in God or in tradition that are the alternatives to rational control. The result is dependence on government together with contempt for government—just what we have now.

Big Government is often contrasted with reliance on the free market, liberals being proponents of the former, conservatives of the latter. That contrast is of course correct, but government and free market are alike in serving the end of rational control, the management of risk. This suggests that conservatives today are, like liberals, committed to the modern idea of rational control. But as opposed to Big Government, the market provides management of risk with allowance for taking a risk. In this regard one might ask, who is the conservative—the entrepreneur who takes a risk or the conservative investor who avoids it?

The market is more of a mechanism than Big Government; it offers rational control without rational controllers. But is that really so? What of stock market advisors; are they not comparable to the social scientists who facilitate Big Government? As Big Government is rational control, rational controllers need science enabling them to control things previously left to nature or chance. Yet stock market advisors typically say that everything depends on the level of risk you are comfortable with; you should not buy risky stocks if they keep you from sleeping at night. Thus it appears that there are irrational dispositions underlying rational control which must be accepted as authoritative even by rational controllers. Some people have conservative dispositions, others not.

What is a conservative disposition? Aristotle describes the conservative dispositions of old people: they are cautious, weak, malicious, unwilling either to hate or to love, small-minded, ungenerous, cowardly, cool, fearful, selfish, more concerned with the useful than the noble, more given to memory than hope, to gain than anger, to calculation than character, to pity than humanity, to querulousness than wit—and they are loquacious.[2] Not a pretty picture! And this is how many people regard conservatives. Aristotle also has a chapter on youth, with its opposite vices. How you are seems to depend a good deal on how close you are to death; and this is fundamental to the idea of risk as well. Aristotle's solution is to say that the mean is the prime of life between the two extremes. He doesn't offer a notion that would discount the benefits of the prime of life throughout one's life (unless that would be what he calls moral virtue). He certainly does his best to reduce the venerableness of the old. Conservatives, despite their love of the old, would do well to avoid the crabbiness of old age.

Despite the unspoken affinity of free-market conservatism for rational control, conservatism mostly doubts the idea of rational control. From David Hume on, conservatives say that the human intellect is not capable of grasping society as a whole so as to reform it. If you attempt to reform everything you will bring on revolution in which the furies of passion, not reason, will triumph. For conservatives reason has its place, which is up close, in front of your nose; the rest they call "nature," that which is beyond human control. Nature can be understood with a single swoop of reason, the whole of nature distinct from humanity as dramatized by romanticism; or nature is left to take care of itself, as guided by the Invisible Hand; or it is said to require reform by increments, as with the notion of prescription in Edmund Burke's thought. In sum, conservatives as defenders of liberalism are aware of its defects, which are: too much reliance on self-interest, causing liberal principles to be vulnerable to charges of selfishness from the left and ignobility from the right; and the related reliance of liberalism on Big Government and rational control.

Bad consequences of the idea of rational control have led conservatives such as the romantic Coleridge, the libertarian Hayek, and the Whig Burke to doubt the value of reason, even in some cases to condemn the use of reason in politics. Instead of universal reason it is better to use prudence in the particulars of each case, and if a general principle is required, let it be historical tradition rather than reason. Yet we have seen that conservatives can be trapped politically in a position of serving the ends of their opponents if they keep solely to the policy of going slow and never think of going back. Conservatives today may find themselves obliged to have recourse to liberal principles when circumstances seem to require vigorous action in order to change an unacceptable situation. One example is the conservative use of the liberal principle of merit in our time in order to oppose affirmative action in promoting racial and gender preferences.

What must conservatives do to defend liberalism from itself? They must defend the liberal regime and the bourgeoisie or middle class, the ruling class of the liberal regime. They must defend what Aristotle might call the interest of the regime. Liberals today and some conservatives are blind to the necessity of maintaining and defending the rulers of the liberal regime. Liberals tend to favor compassion, which means compassion toward enemies of the middle class. They promote welfare or entitlement policies that reward those who lack the sturdy virtues of the liberal middle class, virtues that make compassion possible. Libertarian conservatives, unconcerned for virtue, look to loosen the bonds of responsibility and sacrifice that enable a liberal regime to maintain and defend itself. Postmodern liberal intellectuals, especially, forget that respect for themselves depends on respect for the intellect and for reason. They may be joined by conservative intellectuals of a traditional sort who attack reason, confusing reason with rational control.

Toleration and diversity are liberal policies that conservatives must make compatible with a liberal regime. Liberalism can and must, within reason, tolerate its enemies within a liberal society. But it is not enough to tolerate; conservatives must be alive to diverse contributions to liberalism as a whole. They must see Left and Right not as enemies only but also as permanent tendencies that cannot be got rid of. Conservatives will never kill the Left, for as long as we have a liberal regime the Left will always come back after every defeat. Liberals, believing in progress, are less likely to tolerate conservatives because they are impelled to think that those in the way of progress are prejudiced and do not deserve respect. At the same time, liberals are inclined to relativism, wishing not to judge others. In this mood they maintain that all values are equal, the values of oppressors equal to those of liberals. As progressives liberals are too hard, as relativists they are too soft. Conservatives are both more tolerant and more resistant. They must help out their big brother liberals, who are weaker than conservatives in mind and spirit.

Above all conservatives must defend the liberal form of government that makes liberal politics possible. The liberal form of government has an interest in its own survival, like the Aristotelian regime, but it is also unlike that regime. In the Aristotelian regime the form is the end: for example, the democratic form of government has as its end a democratic way of life. But in the liberal regime the form is partly distinct from the end. In its view the purpose of democracy is partly to live a democratic life, but it is also to secure the rights of life, liberty, and the pursuit of happiness. In liberalism, rights are prior to government and therefore serve as a separate basis by which to judge whether government is doing its job well. We see a sign of this in the question that our politicians often pose to the electorate: Are you better off?

Being better off is distinct from being a better democrat; it is a separate, nonpolitical standard that a liberal regime adopts for itself and with which it invites support. As such, it can be used against a liberal regime that does not deliver on its promises. For the Aristotelian regime there is no such problem in maintaining the form of government, but the problem is to restrain the tendency of any form of government to intensify itself, to make itself more extreme. A liberal regime, however, must struggle to maintain its form of government because it is always being judged against the standard of an end that is outside itself. Its end is not so much democracy as a form of government as it is equal rights or plain and simple equality for all men everywhere—that is, human rights. This is what Tocqueville meant when he spoke of democracy as a continuing democratic revolution. A liberal democracy hurtles forward toward more democracy without considering whether more democracy is in the interest of a liberal regime.

Feminism is an example of this recklessness, for it desires the abolition of sex roles but does not look carefully at society to see how this would work. How will families stay together when there is constant dispute between the sexes as to what is an equal share for each? Equality in an abstract sense is democratization without attending to what keeps liberal democracy a viable form of government. It seems that a democratic society in the process of democratization has no idea of where it is going. After civil rights for blacks we discovered equal rights for women, and after these, equal rights for gays. Each stage of equalization failed to notice what had been left undone, hence failed to foresee what needed to be done. What is the next item of inequality, now unappreciated, that suddenly we will see must be rectified? Could it be equal rights for the ugly? Or for the stupid? These inequalities are weighty and consequential, capable of arousing indignation yet not easy to erase.

The Form of Conservatism

Now we may ask what is the liberal form of government? It is limited government as opposed to Big Government, constitutional government in a new, non-Aristotelian sense. This constitutional government is to be found in the U.S. Constitution, and its principles are expounded in the writings of the American framers and founders. Above all, they are found in *The Federalist* and in Tocqueville's *Democracy in America* (for Tocqueville, a Frenchman, is America's critic and mentor). Neither of these works speaks of "conservatism," yet they should be considered more authoritative today for conservatism than any or all of the expressly conservative writers who have written more recently, however welcome and convincing they may be.

These two books are conservative in the deep sense of coming from within America. They do not adopt a theoretical stance of judging America from the outside according to the demands of a theory, especially the abstract theory of liberalism. The abstract theory starts from the very unconservative premise of the state of nature, a start from the very beginning before there is any society or civilization. *The Federalist*, however, starts from the political situation of the free, republican American people. That particular people is unable to govern itself effectively and needs a new instrument. Publius (purported author of *The Federalist*, whose name comes from a Roman popular statesman, not a writer or philosopher) takes up the formal provisions of the governmental structure in the new Constitution and expounds the reasons why they have been framed as they are.

Thus American constitutionalism comes out of the Constitution, a practical solution for a political crisis, rather than from arguments by theorists of liberty. (The most praised theorist in *The Federalist* is the "celebrated Montesquieu," the greatest modern student of comparative government and the least abstract of liberal thinkers.) The Constitution has its own principles, departing in some important particulars from those of liberal or republican thinkers, as when it insists on the necessity of a strong executive and on the advantages of an "extended sphere," a large republic. In addition are the famous compromises in the Constitution, defended as such in terms that reject mere theoretical consistency. On several occasions Publius expresses his distaste for political abstractions and extreme formulations. All this is conservatism in practice, where one would expect and hope to find it, if not conservatism in name.

In *Democracy in America* Tocqueville shows a similar dislike for abstract liberal theory. He does not mention the abstract, liberal grounding of politics in the state of nature, but instead describes the "point of departure" of American democracy in the ideas and practices of a particular group, the Puritans. He reveals the bad influence of liberal and conservative theorists who conceive liberty and religion to be in perpetual mutual antagonism, and he denounces theoretical pantheists and "democratic historians" for their malign exaggeration of democratic tendencies. His own insights are presented as things he saw in America, not as conceptual inventions of his own: the American facility for joining together in civil and political associations, the American town meeting, and, of course, the American Constitution. Here again, though we do not see the word "conservatism," we see the conservative spirit of distrust of liberal theory in partnership with an appreciation for the customs and mores of democratic liberty in the actual practice of a particular regime.

The American Constitution provides popular government because the government is chosen by the people, yet government is also withdrawn from the people so that the people can judge it in democratic elections. In a democratic election the people choose the government and judge the same government they choose. The people are both responsible for the government they choose and not responsible when they draw back to judge it. If they vote out the existing government they do not apologize for their own bad choice in the preceding election. They are the sovereign, and sovereigns do not blame themselves, nor do they apologize.

The interest of a liberal regime is in the defense of the *forms* of the constitution; this is what defending liberalism means. Those forms put obstacles between the people's will and the government's actions so that the people's will has to be expressed constitutionally. This means, for example, that an unpopular government has to be voted out of office; it cannot, it should not be shamed into retirement by low ratings in the polls. Government is withdrawn from the people for two opposite reasons: so that the people are forced to act on their own and so that the government can act on its own. The people acting on their own are in voluntary association (the good sense of populism) rather than resting inactive as consumers, clients, or dependents of Big Government. If the people are dependents, they have too strong an interest in continuing the dole they live on. They cannot imagine living otherwise and are difficult to rouse from complacent acceptance of what seems to them costless. Their energy declines as they turn their attention away from the public to the private affairs of themselves and their intimates. True populism, however, avoids dependence on Big Government and manipulation by demagogues. A healthy democratic people does not wait for things to be done for it but organizes its affairs, not of course without prompting from its leaders, in associations of its own making. This is the democracy Tocqueville found *in* America.

The government acting on its own can control the people.[3] Within what might be called its "constitutional space," it can maintain its ability to call for forbearance, even sacrifice, from the people. In the Constitution control of the people is located in the executive and judicial powers more than in Congress, which is elected in order to respond to the people's will. Actually the six-year term of office for the Senate (and in the original Constitution its election by state legislatures) was designed to distinguish it from the House of Representatives, which with its two-year term and direct election is closer to the popular will. The judiciary, derived from the people but not elected by them, has a necessary distance from popular will. When by "judicial review" the judiciary affirms the constitutionality of legislation, it enforces a higher law than ordinary law. The higher law is what the people once willed when they ratified the Constitution. Publius can claim that when the Supreme Court rejects a law duly passed, it is honoring the people's will in its permanent aspect over its temporary wishes. Still, this judicial power is a very real restriction on the sovereignty of the people's will.

The executive, too, is at a distance from the people, and for the sake of two distinct functions. Under the Constitution the executive is not a committee (as with previous republics, including America under the Articles of Confederation) but a single person; it is the monarchical presence in our system. One-man rule is good for dealing with emergencies, when circumstances require a quick, unopposed reaction, as after the attacks on Pearl Harbor in

1941 and on the World Trade Center in 2001. But it is also required to set and follow a long-term course of policy, one of the "extensive and arduous enterprises" that Publius attributes to the executive function, such as Franklin Roosevelt's New Deal or George W. Bush's foreign policy of preemptive war. Publius stresses the "personal firmness" of the president, called forth by a four-year term repeatable without limit (in the original Constitution), enabling him to avoid an attitude of "servile pliancy" to the immediate wishes of the people. *The Federalist* does not have a favorable view of "leadership," which it considers to be a euphemism for irresponsible followership. A strong president in its opinion is strong against dangerous currents of whimsicality and haste in popular judgments, not "strong" in the sense of taking the people where they may incontinently want to go. An active but demagogic president of the latter tendency would be considered weak.

Publius presents a new virtue that will guide the behavior of American statesmen who have the advantage of constitutional space.[4] This is the virtue of responsibility, and it has succeeded so well in American democracy that it has become the chief virtue, public and private, of our time. Publius introduces it in regard to the Senate and the presidency (*Federalist* 63 and 70). For him it is a public virtue of republican government, referring to the relationship between a public official and the people. It means that the official should not only be accountable or responsive to the people—and before *The Federalist*, this was the sole meaning given to "responsible"—but also act effectively on their behalf. Responsible politicians act for the people, doing what the people cannot do for themselves but can judge afterwards in speaking, associating, and voting.

Our constitutional government combines populism and elitism, both understood, we now see, in a healthy way. Its populism is intended to preserve the forms of consent, especially elections, against the temptation to govern through the polls or to welcome the intrusions of judicial activism. Its elitism is designed to keep a distance between people and government, not to encourage the arbitrary exercise of power but on the contrary to enable government to act consistently and on principle—that is, responsibly. This alliance opposes a contrary combination of unhealthy populism and elitism: the populism that wants unending democratization and the elitism that also wants this without regard to the people's needs, especially the need to get their consent.

For conservatives, preserving the forms of popular consent means insisting on constitutional due process; it is the conservative strategy of going slow. Keeping a distance between government and people, however, allows a conservative government to act on principle. To be a conservative is a balancing act. You have to compromise so as to get the consent of a majority, and you have to uphold the principle of restoring our Constitution, our limited government, with the support of that majority.

Based on the Constitution and its tradition—legal, political, and intellectual—conservatism in America should be American in origin, style, and content. Conservatives may of course draw from foreign sources—I yield to no one in the admiration due to Edmund Burke, a great friend of America—but they should be read with a view to possibilities in America. America cannot abandon the great principles of liberalism, above all the principle of self-government and, with it, the constitutional means for achieving and preserving it. America cannot abandon the ambition that accompanies the principle stated on the first page of *The Federalist* of making an experiment in self-government in which all mankind has an interest. This ambition has been restated by many American statesmen, and by none so nobly as Abraham Lincoln. Lincoln has deservedly become a focus of American conservatives, who explain his actions and defend them against petty detractors.[5] Their works, together with studies of the American founders and other American statesmen, nurture and refresh the combination of patriotism and philanthropy peculiar to American constitutionalism.

American conservatives should take pride not only in what their country has accomplished but even more in what it has meant to accomplish. This is not to deny the danger of over-ambition from imperialism, which is the true ambition of serving as an example to other peoples distorted and perverted into tyranny. But lack of ambition has its risk, too, in failing (as we say) to meet our responsibilities. In view of the high ambition of the American Founding, Americans cannot say that they do not care for the exertions necessary to greatness, that they have had greatness thrust upon them, and that they wish it would go away.

Ambition in this high sense goes with responsibility as the virtue of statesmen who occupy "constitutional space." This combination is the motive that makes the separation of powers work, for in *Federalist* 51 we are told that "ambition must be made to counteract ambition." Ambition is surely self-interested, because an ambitious person is eager for honor and honor for himself. But according to Aristotle, it is in right measure also a virtue. This means that, though it is voluntary, it is not merely spontaneous, requiring no effort, arising from untutored self-interest. Since the Constitution does not work mechanically, it is in need of virtue. The need for virtue is not confined to the Founding or to times of crisis, because we do not know when crises will come, and we can lose the capacity for meeting them by drifting along in lazy routine. Every generation needs our American, constitutional virtue, and we conservatives should never let it go out of style.

5

The Electoral Future of Conservatism

Michael Barone

ALMOST TWENTY-FIVE YEARS AGO, in the first months of the Reagan administration, while attending a conference on the problems facing America I found myself talking with a young Republican congressman who had had some experience in the executive branch. Those were the days when the conventional wisdom was that America's best days were behind us. We were told by respected experts that America could no longer have low-inflation economic growth; it was simply impossible, and that people should adjust themselves to continued low growth and high inflation. We were told by respected experts that America was in retreat in the world, that the Soviet Union and the Third World were rising forces with which we should hope to reach some kind of accommodation even as we were in retreat. The young congressman agreed that we were in desperate times. Ronald Reagan had announced bold new policies, but neither he nor I were at all sure they would work. I sure hope they do, I remember him saying, or words to that effect, "We've really got to somehow turn things around. But I'm not sure we can make it."

That young congressman was Dick Cheney, then in his second term as the single representative from Wyoming, first elected after his stint as President Gerald Ford's chief of staff. In the years since, we know what has happened. America has had low inflation economic growth almost continuously since the Reagan tax cuts were implemented. America surged to victory in the Cold

War and emerged as the single global superpower. The conservative ideas that the respected experts of twenty-five years ago dismissed out of hand have been exonerated in the hard world of experience. And events have proved that, as Ronald Reagan liked to say, America's best days are ahead of us.

Similarly, conservative ideas have prevailed in elections. Republicans have won five of the last seven presidential elections, four with an absolute majority of the vote. Democrats have won two, neither time with an absolute majority of the vote. Before 2006, Republicans had the last six congressional elections, a record equaled only once before, in 1918–28 and surpassed only in 1860–74 and 1894–1910. Incidentally, for those in the mainstream media who think that opposition to abortion is politically fatal, in the nine presidential elections since *Roe v. Wade*, the more antiabortion candidate has won seven times.

Why a Bright Future?

So what is the electoral future of conservatism? I think that, for all the challenges that others in this volume have identified for the conservative coalition, conservatism's electoral fortunes are pretty good—certainly better than the electoral future of liberalism. Even more fascinating is that we seem to be in an era of political stasis, in which the balance of power between the parties remains very much the same and the contours of support, in states and districts and among demographic groups, has also remained very much the same. This has been true for almost exactly ten years, since the 1995–96 budget showdown between Newt Gingrich and Bill Clinton. The cast of characters may have changed, but voter preferences appear to have stayed pretty much the same.

The last decade, then, has been a period of sharp polarization and of rough equality between the parties, with, I would argue, a modest advantage for the Republicans. It is also a period when we have seen a convergence in electoral behavior between presidential and congressional vote choice. Ticket-splitting was quite common between the 1960s and up through 1992 for a number of reasons, the least of which was a Democratic Party with distinct northern and southern wings. But since 1994 ticket-splitting has largely disappeared, especially with the secular realignment of the once solid Democratic South to the Republican column. The numbers do not lie. In 1996 Bill Clinton was reelected with 49 percent of the vote and the Republicans won the national popular vote tally for the House by 49 to 48.5 percent. In 1998, the impeachment year, Republicans won the popular vote for the House by 49 to 48 percent. In 2000 the presidential election was tied, 48 to 48 percent, and the Republicans won the popular vote for the House by 49 to 48 percent. In 2002, with George W. Bush's job approval rating still sky high in the wake of 9/11, Republicans won the popular vote for the House by 51 to 47 percent, bucking the usual trend for midterm losses for the president's party in Congress. In 2004 Bush, with only about a 50 percent job approval rating, was reelected by a 51 to 48 percent margin, and the Republicans won the popular vote for the House by 50 to 46 percent.

On balance these numbers show a very small but still decided advantage for the Republicans—an advantage which has given them the White House for the last two terms and majorities in the House and Senate for most of those years. From 1994–2004, the Republicans have won between 49 and 51 percent of the vote in House elections, and the Democrats have won between 46 and 48.5 percent of the vote during the same period. In presidential elections Republicans have won between 48 and 51 percent of the vote and Democrats between 48 and 49 percent of the vote (I leave aside Bob Dole's 41 percent in 1996; polling indicated that he was the second choice of the bulk of the 8 percent who voted for Ross Perot in that election cycle, in which case Dole's percentage would have been about 47 percent, quite consistent with the averages of the period).

Note that Bill Clinton in 1996 and Al Gore in 2000 were running as the candidates of the incumbent party in times of apparent peace and apparent prosperity—the best posture for an aspiring candidate. Yet they won the same 49 and 48 percent of the vote that we have seen throughout this period of deadlock. George W. Bush was running in 2004 as the candidate of the incumbent party in a time not of peace and, in the perception of most voters anyway, not of prosperity. Yet he did a bit better, with 51 percent of the vote. I think that with today's polarized electorate there is a ceiling on the Democrats' vote just a little above 50 percent. I think there is also a ceiling on the Republican vote, but that it is around the low-to-mid 50s—which is what John McCain is currently receiving in preliminary polls against Hillary Rodham Clinton.

Note also that these numbers are not at all responsive to economic conditions or to the job approval or favorability ratings of the parties' leading figures. In 1996, Bill Clinton and his party ran far below his job approval numbers, and House Republicans ran far ahead of Newt Gingrich's favorability ratings (the same was the case in 1998 for both Democratic and Republican congressional candidates when compared to Clinton and Gingrich's job approval ratings). Similarly, Al Gore ran well below Clinton's job approval rating in 2000, and House Republicans in 2002 ran well below Bush's then high job approval. In 2002 House Republicans, the incumbent party, made gains despite a poor economy, and in 2004 Bush and House Republicans ran well ahead of the ratings of the economy. Overall, whether you are talking about the approval ratings of Bill Clinton or George W. Bush, Newt Gingrich or Tom Daschle, it would appear that each side seems to be stuck within the same range of voter support.

It is well known by now that voters are divided more along cultural lines than along economic lines. Greenwich, Connecticut, where George W. Bush's grandfather was first selectman for twenty years, and which has a median housing price of something like $2.6 million, voted only 54 percent for Bush in 2004. The Upper East Side of Manhattan and the West Side of Los Angeles, also quite affluent, voted heavily for John Kerry. In contrast, Bush swept the South and the Great Plains, where incomes are lower than the national average. The demographic variable that is now most highly correlated with voting behavior is religion—or intensity of religion. White Evangelical Protestants and Mormons voted more than 70 percent for Bush. Jews and seculars voted more than 70 percent for Kerry. Within each religious group, those who attend services more regularly are more likely than others to have voted for Bush; even among black Protestants the Bush vote increased somewhat in some states, notably Ohio. Hispanic Catholics voted for Kerry, but Hispanic Protestants—a growing group—voted for Bush.

It has long been the mantra of some Democratic strategists that Republicans cannot win if turnout is increased and the electorate expanded. But Bush ran better than Clinton or Gore despite—or rather because—of a vast expansion of the electorate. Total turnout in 2004 was up 16 percent over 2000—a rise only seen in four other elections in the preceding 108 years, except for those when women gained the franchise. With this expansion, John Kerry's popular vote was also up a significant 16 percent over Al Gore's in 2000. But George W. Bush's popular vote total went up even more, a whopping 23 percent increase between 2000 and 2004. That is a truly historic increase, of the sort that Franklin Roosevelt achieved between 1932 and 1936. In 2004, the total electorate expanded from 105 million to 122 million, with Bush receiving twelve million more votes in the process. By way of contrast, when Bill Clinton was reelected the electorate actually contracted from 104 million to 96 million, and his own vote total increased by a much smaller amount, roughly two million votes.

Why a Democratic Majority Is Not Emerging

There are some keen observers of American politics that have recently maintained that growing segments of the electorate will eventually move away from conservatives and Republicans and toward liberals and Democrats, creating an emerging Democratic majority. That majority of course has yet to emerge, but if it did, it would do so because a rising tide of Latinos and culturally liberal young people would replace and outvote the prebaby boom generation and white segments of the electorate, which have declined as a percentage of the electorate according to recent demographic trends. However,

Michael Barone

this assumes that Latinos will stay solidly in the Democratic camp, something that certainly did not happen in 2004. In that presidential election, Latinos, according to the most reliable exit polls, voted 45 percent for George W. Bush, the highest Latino support for a Republican presidential candidate ever. In other words, they voted more like whites than like blacks. As for young voters, Bush did do poorly among those under twenty-five—a problem Republicans and conservatives need to address. But given the small percentage of the electorate historically occupied by younger voters, this weakness did not spell electoral defeat for the president.

Another political trend also tends to undermine the emerging Democratic majority thesis. In the 100 counties with populations above 10,000 that had the greatest percentage population increase between 2000 and 2004—in other words, the 100 fastest growing counties—Bush carried 97. These counties accounted for 25 percent of the nation's total population increase from 2000 to 2004. Bush carried these 100 counties by 1,815,000 votes—more than half his national popular vote plurality. These are by and large exurban counties, counties at the outer edge of metropolitan areas, counties where subdivisions are growing up at freeway interchanges, with sparkling new shopping malls and giant megachurches, where parents are raising young families. They are not the precincts of the wealthy elite, such as Greenwich, Connecticut, where real estate values are sky high and, because of restrictions on growth and development, population increase is minimal. Given these dynamics, even if Republican candidates continue to underperform in traditional affluent suburban neighborhoods, the GOP's growing power in the exurbs has the potential to more than compensate for this decline in a formerly dependable voting bloc.

Challenges to the Conservative Republican Hegemony

Looking ahead, of course the current static pattern of party preferences will change—but I have seen no signs yet that convince me that it has happened yet. And I do not think it is certain that any change will benefit the Democrats or the liberals in the longrun. In the current environment, the chief danger to Republican and conservative success is low turnout. For that reason, it is worrying that conservative elites and conservatives around the country have started to express dissatisfaction with the Bush administration and the Republican record—over spending, over immigration, over the Harriet Miers nomination, and especially over the handling of the Iraq War. If the conservative base becomes dispirited or disillusioned, like it did in 2006, conservative turnout will fall, leading to Republican defeat at the hands of an energized Democratic base.

Yet on the whole I think Republicans hold the better hand. The Republican base is largely united, not just on George W. Bush but on issues. Economic conservatives and cultural conservatives have no major goals which are in conflict; the conflict, if there is any, is over what issues should be emphasized. It is true that during the 1990s Republicans lost many voters on cultural issues in the suburbs, especially the affluent suburbs of the largest metropolitan areas in the country. But they have continued to win despite those losses. In addition, the Republican electorate continues to believe that we are in danger and that we need a strong national defense and a president who will take strong steps to protect us. It is not entirely a coincidence that the only time in the last quarter-century that Democratic presidential candidates have won a plurality of the popular vote—and in no case did that rise to a majority—was in the years between the end of the Cold War and September 11.

The Democrats, in contrast, are a split party—among both their politicians and their voters. On one hand there are Democrats who believe in American exceptionalism, the idea that this country is special and especially good, an idea shared by Democrats like Roosevelt, Truman, and Kennedy and enunciated on occasion by Bill Clinton. On the other hand are Democrats who have what Harvard professor Samuel Huntington calls transnational loyalties, who believe that this country is no better than any other, and in many respects is decidedly worse. These are the Democrats who, through Howard Dean's candidacy, set the tone for the battle for the party's nomination in 2004 and who are setting it today, in controversies ranging from Supreme Court nominations to NSA surveillance of al-Qaeda phone calls to the U.S. It is no accident that John Kerry said, "I actually did vote for the $87 billion before I voted against it." He was trying to rally both halves of a deeply divided party. That is a difficult task, as Kerry showed. It takes a politician with the transcendent political skills of a Bill Clinton to do it. It is not clear that the Democratic Party has a candidate with those skills for 2008.

I also think that the presidential candidate can make a difference. In the 1980s Ronald Reagan proved a significantly more widely acceptable candidate than either Bill Clinton or George W. Bush has done. He was reelected with 59 percent of the vote and carried forty-nine states; he carried New York and Massachusetts twice. I think one reason that Reagan was able to attract such wide support is that he could draw on the universal popular cultures with which he had grown up and in which he made his prepolitical career—radio of the 1920s and 1930s, movies of the 1930s and 1940s, television of the 1950s. Today, in contrast, we do not have such a universal popular culture; instead we have various popular cultures, with niche audiences. And our two baby boomer presidents have appealed to different niches—and are absolutely loathed by those on the other side of the cultural divide. Bill Clinton personifies the liberal half of the baby boom generation, though he also can speak in the language of religious Christians. George W. Bush personifies the conservative half of the baby boom generation, and he has shown, in public at least, little facility to speak an idiom that resonates with the other half.

Would a different Republican presidential candidate, one less identified with cultural conservatism—John McCain, perhaps, or Rudy Giuliani—be less polarizing? Would a different kind of Democratic candidate, one less identified with cultural liberalism—NASCAR-loving Mark Warner, perhaps—be less polarizing? I think that is possible. But a McCain or Giuliani nomination would also tend to end the conflation of conservatism and the Republican Party, and it is unclear whether such a candidate could rally high turnout from some key constituencies—the small towns and rural counties of Ohio or Missouri, for example—as much as George W. Bush did in 2004. Nor is it clear that a candidate like Warner could rally the Democrats' left-wing transnational base, or hold votes against a left-wing third candidate.

Conservatives have some reason already to be disappointed with the Bush and Republican record. Economic conservatives have reason to be disappointed at the continued growth of government. Cultural conservatives have reason to be disappointed at the fact that abortion policy continues unchanged and that the culture in some respects continues to deteriorate. But, as President Bush has pointed out in important ways the culture is changing for the better. Back in the days when Adlai Stevenson was talking about the liberal hour, there was a general assumption—shared by the founders of *National Review*—that history must always move to the left. Today, thanks largely to the successes of American conservatism, that assumption seems to have been disproved. It is widely accepted, as it was not when I was in college, that markets work and morals matter. And so I think the electoral future of a movement that believes those things is likely to be pretty good—even if, in this world, its success must always be incomplete.

6

Conservatism, Democracy, and Foreign Policy

Daniel J. Mahoney

IN A PENETRATING ESSAY dating from 1948, the Hungarian political philosopher Aurel Kolnai wrote that in our time, a balanced defense of liberty should aim "to *displace the spiritual stress* from the 'common man' aspect of Democracy to its aspect of constitutionalism and of moral continuity with the high tradition of Antiquity, Christendom, and the half-surviving Liberal cultures of yesterday."[1] Kolnai's profoundly conservative appreciation of the moral foundations of democracy provides a principled ground for resisting what Roger Scruton has called "the culture of repudiation" and for making one's way in the culture wars. Kolnai's thought can also provide inspiration for a principled and prudent foreign policy that does not confuse a robust defense of liberty with doctrinaire support for democracy abroad. An early critic of both National Socialism and Soviet communism, Kolnai knew that the Western world has every reason to consider totalitarianism the *summum malum*, the worst political evil. But a variety of legitimate anti-totalitarian political options exist even in a "democratic" age. In foreign policy, the intellectual alternatives are not exhausted by cultural relativism, on the one hand, and a democratic "progressivism" that overlooks the fragility of political civilization, on the other.

In my view, the West's victory over communism is best understood not as a victory for democracy per se—especially not for democracy in its current, postnational and postreligious manifestation—but rather, as a defeat for the utopian illusion that human beings could somehow live free and dignified lives without property, religion, nations, or politics. The collapse of Soviet communism was thus the definitive repudiation of what the Hegelio-Marxist philosopher Alexandre Kojève called "the universal and homogenous state." Kojève believed that by the mid-twentieth century the avant-garde of humanity had put "an end to history," to all world-transforming political or ideological contestation. Henceforth, there would be no politics, only the administration of things, whether by communist commissars or EU bureaucrats. This was history's *inevitable* denouement. These fantasies ought to have been revealed for what they were by the *annus mirabilis* 1989.

Yet such is the hold of historicism on us that politicians and theorists across the ideological spectrum succumbed to the temptation to give a "progressivist" interpretation of the end of the Cold War itself. Marvelously mirroring Marxist arguments, lifelong anticommunists now claimed that it was the West's victory in the Cold War that had been inevitable, that communism was destined to collapse because it had been "on the wrong side of History." In his address to the British parliament in 1982, Ronald Reagan had stated that "the Soviet Union . . . runs against the tide of history by denying freedom and human dignity to its citizens." Surely this noble statesman was correct that communism entailed nothing less than a fundamental assault on "the natural order of things." But it was another matter to turn the tables on the Marxists by claiming that "History" favored the universal triumph of the democratic ideal. With the systematic breakdown of classical and Christian education in the Western world, few were still capable of articulating an older wisdom that refused to identify the Good with the alleged movement of History.

With the publication of Francis Fukuyama's article "The End of History?" in The *National Interest* in 1989 (and the book that quickly followed on its heels), the world was treated to a sophisticated neo-"Marxist" interpretation of the fall of communism, this time at the service of a broadly conservative politics. According to Fukuyama, the end of the Cold War had indeed culminated in something like the "universal and homogenous state." But in one of those displays of dialectical cleverness beloved by social theorists, democratic capitalism was now said to alone embody the authentic "recognition of man by man." In a "Ruse of Reason" worthy of Hegel himself, History had vindicated the bourgeois order whose doom had been prophesied by a century and a half of "progressive" thought.

Fukuyama's thesis gave powerful impetus to what can be called the "second neoconservatism," an intellectual current that wished to follow up the defeat of communism with vigorous support for a "global democratic revolution" aided and sustained by the military and political power of the United States. The first neoconservatism, in contrast to the second, had been more anti-

Daniel J. Mahoney

totalitarian than "democratic" in orientation, and was perfectly willing to acknowledge the sheer intractability of cultures and civilizations. Whatever the intellectual pedigree of some of its adherents, the new neoconservatism owed more to Alexandre Kojève than to Leo Strauss, who had been an unremitting critic of the "universal and homogenous state" in all its forms. The new neoconservatism shared few of the older neoconservatism's concerns about the pernicious spiritual and cultural effects of a fully "democratized" polity and culture (see almost any essay by Irving Kristol from the 1970s) or its hesitations about dogmatic support for human rights in foreign policy (the *locus classicus* of this position is Jeane J. Kirkpatrick's important 1979 *Commentary* essay, "Dictatorships and Double Standards").

Fukuyama's Indictment

In his latest book, *America at the Crossroads: Democracy, Power, and the Neoconservative Legacy* (2006), Fukuyama ignores his own role in the genesis of the "second neoconservatism." In important respects, the present-day partisans of "muscular Wilsonianism" have built upon Fukuyaman premises about "the end of history" and the unchallenged ideological ascendancy of liberal democracy, even if they have emphasized the efficacy of military power more than Fukuyama now thinks prudent. In his current self-presentation, Fukuyama plays Marx to William Kristol's Lenin. He defends the desirability and ultimate inevitability of global democratization while criticizing ill-advised efforts to push the process along. He sees himself as the true neoconservative, one who has remained faithful to neoconservatism's original critique of large-scale social engineering and its salutary concern about the unintended consequences of social action. In his new book and in the postscript to the 2005 edition of *The End of History and the Last Man*, Fukuyama defends a relatively uncontroversial version of modernization theory that owes more to Tocqueville and Weber than to Kojève. He claims that he "never posited a strong version of modernization theory, with rigid stages of development or economically determined outcomes. Contingency, leadership, and ideas always play a complicating role, which make major setbacks possible if not likely."

There is an element of truth, as well as much bad faith, in these formulations. The second neoconservatism is, to be sure, more activist than anything suggested in Fukuyama's original speculations about the nature of the post–Cold War world. But just as Leninist voluntarism—the revolutionary effort to give History a shove toward its ultimate destination—was a natural consequence of Marx's own philosophy of history, so Fukuyama's announcement of the ideological triumph of liberal democracy was bound to provide inspiration for what was to become the second neoconservatism. Fukuyama cannot evade responsibility for his decisive role in interpreting the collapse of communism in an essentially progressivist or historicist light. It is also difficult to understand why Fukuyama needed to resort to an obscure mélange of Hegel and Kojève, or to rhetoric about the "end of history," if all he had in mind from the beginning was a relatively innocuous version of modernization theory. This born-again Tocquevillian now more carefully distinguishes between economic and social modernization (which indeed has something "irresistible" about it) and political liberty, which can never simply be guaranteed by unfolding historical or social processes. To make that distinction, however, is to deny any *essential* identification of modernization with "the end of history." It is to affirm with Tocqueville and the ancients that the political problem is in principle unsolvable, that History can never substitute for the imperative for human beings "to put reasons and actions in common," as Aristotle put it.

In addition to his failure to appreciate the tendentious logic of his own position, Fukuyama's attribution of real or even metaphorical Leninism both to the Bush administration and to contemporary neoconservatives is unjust and irresponsible. It muddies the theoretical waters while adding nothing to our understanding of the real alternatives facing citizens and statesmen today. Leninism entailed a self-conscious abrogation of the moral law in the name of a revolutionary project to create a New Man and a New Society. It was a manifestation of an inhuman ideological impulse that Edmund Burke did not hesitate to call (in different historical circumstances) "metaphysical madness." Leninism inevitably gave rise to totalitarianism because its ends were *contra naturum* and because it provided ideological justification for tyranny and terror on a truly unprecedented scale. Neoconservatives such as William Kristol may overstate the universal appeal of "democracy" and the role that American power can play in promoting it around the world. That is surely a question for debate and discussion. But they are decent men who have never claimed that moral considerations can be suspended in pursuit of utopian ends.

Moreover, the neoconservatives are wrestling with a real problem made more pressing by the terrorist attacks of September 11, 2001—namely, the multiple ways in which social stagnation and political authoritarianism conspire to reinforce fanaticism throughout the Arab Islamic world. And however "muscular" their approach to foreign policy, they have not advocated the indiscriminate use of military power or succumbed to the illusion that democracy can simply be imposed from "the barrel of a gun." To suggest otherwise is to engage in wild caricatures of a serious, if flawed, approach to the conduct of American foreign policy.

There is thus something unhinged about John Gray's recent suggestion in the pages of The *American Interest* (Summer 2006) that "neoconservatism" represents the continuation of the Marxist-Leninist project and that it will inevitably lead to the same tragic consequences. These extreme formulations—worthy of an ideologue and not a political philosopher—would be easy to dismiss if they did not also recur with alarming regularity in "realist" and "paleoconservative" criticisms of neoconservatism in general, and the Bush foreign policy in particular. President Bush is the first conservative president to be regularly castigated as a "Jacobin" and "Leninist" by a significant number of critics within the conservative intellectual community. Such criticisms paradoxically obscure the genuine weaknesses of the Bush Doctrine by attributing mere fanaticism to a foreign policy that in truth has equal measures of strength and weakness.

A Neoconservative Foreign Policy?

The critics of current American foreign policy tend to presuppose that the Bush administration is carrying out a plan of action that was designed in advance by neoconservative intellectuals. In this view, President Bush is somehow a captive of a cabal of ex-leftist Jewish intellectuals, students of Leo Strauss, and a group of writers and thinkers around William Kristol's *Weekly Standard*. It is conveniently forgotten or ignored that none of the principals in the administration is a neoconservative—with the arguable exception of Vice President Cheney, who indeed moved closer to neoconservative positions during his tenure at the American Enterprise Institute in the 1990s. It must be remembered that neoconservative advocates of a militarily assertive neo-Wilsonian foreign policy were initially wary of George W. Bush and tended to support the internationalist John McCain in the 2000 Republican primaries. As a candidate, Bush repeatedly expressed his suspicion of humanitarian interventions abroad and called for greater "humility" in the conduct of American foreign policy. The first eight months of the Bush presidency were dedicated to a domestic agenda of "compassionate conservatism" centered around education reform and "faith-based initiatives." Bush's initial instincts about foreign policy—he did not articulate anything as systematic as a doctrine or a grand strategy—were undoubtedly unilateralist, but they were by no means unduly interventionist. In this regard at least, 9/11 did indeed "change everything."

Bush never became a neoconservative—he operates too much on an instinctual plane to join an intellectual party of any sort—but he formed a tactical alliance with those who provided a theoretical rationale for a more assertive foreign policy. The so-called Bush Doctrine "called for offensive operations, including preemptive war, against terrorists and their abetters, more specifically, against the regimes that had sponsored, encouraged, or merely tolerated, any 'terrorist group of global reach.'"[2] If preemptive action (not necessarily of a military sort) against terror-supporting "rogue states" was the weapon of choice of the new strategic doctrine, the promotion of democratic "regime change" provided the moral compass for a foreign policy that aimed to take the fight to an unscrupulous and nihilistic enemy. Its proponents vigorously defended support for democratic transformation in the Middle East as a new kind of realism rather than an ideological crusade motivated by abstract or utopian considerations.

It is hard to deny that this overall project is informed by a strong dose of realism and contains no small element of daring and moral nobility. For too long the United States coddled corrupt, autocratic regimes in the Middle East as long as they kept the oil flowing or served our strategic interests. The new approach provided a comprehensive framework for navigating the post-9/11 world and a sense of mission to an America that had been awakened from her somnolence by the surprise assault on our national soil. President Bush was no doubt inspired by the idea of striking at the very sources of tyranny and terror in the Arab Islamic world. But his decency and respect for common humanity, undeniable virtues in a democratic statesman, led him to exaggerate the prospects for self-government in a region where secular and religious authoritarianism too often compete to shape the destinies of peoples. In addition, President Bush is a moralist who clearly relishes an unequivocal confrontation with political evil. He is inclined to see any qualification of doctrinaire universalism as a choice for "relativism" rather than a salutary recognition of the undeniable *fact* that self-government has crucial historical, moral, cultural, and spiritual prerequisites.

Strengths and Limits of the New Approach

The Bush administration is not wrong, of course, to recognize important parallels between Jihadist radicalism and the political religions of the twentieth century. Whatever the differences between the "pious cruelty" of the Islamists and the atheistic tyrannies of the twentieth century, both ideological currents disdained bourgeois democracy and repudiated the moral law in the name of ostensibly more sublime aspirations and goals. In his latest book, however, Fukuyama rightfully questions whether Islamism poses the same kind of "existential threat" to Western civilization that was posed by communism and Nazism. With its open contempt for rationality, civil society, and ordinary morality, and its disdain for less virulent currents of Islam, Jihadist extremism mainly appeals to the marginal and dislocated, to those who have been uprooted by the whirlwinds of globalization. It will never attract the sympathy of Western intellectuals as communism did during the long social crisis that dominated the first half of the twentieth century. The West must prepare itself for a protracted struggle with a fanatical international movement that aspires to force the whole of humanity to live within "the house of Islam." With such a movement there can be no compromise or negotiated settlement. Still, it is difficult to argue that in this struggle the West's very existence—or the moral legitimacy of liberal democracy—is genuinely at stake.

To be sure, any adequate response to the terrorist threat demands a mixture of civic and martial fortitude and political dexterity that goes far beyond the anemic police measures favored by quasi-pacifistic Europeans today. But inexact talk about an open-ended "War on Terror"—which in truth implies war without end—does not adequately convey the unsettling gray zone between war and peace that will characterize the international situation for the foreseeable future. Nor is it self-evident that democracy, especially electoral democracy, can provide the antidote to the Islamist virus.

After 9/11 the Bush administration lost an opportunity to articulate a textured anti-totalitarianism on the model of the old neoconservatism, one that combined principled opposition to despotism with a carefully calibrated politics of prudence. Instead, President Bush increasingly defined the global political alternatives in a starkly Manichean way as a choice between democracy and tyranny. His understanding of the contemporary world rests on a doctrinaire political science that in the end recognizes one and only one path to human freedom and flourishing. This is the downside of a positive feature. As we have seen over the past five years, Bush's clear-sighted recognition of good and evil is the major source of his principled tough-mindedness as a statesman. He is to be applauded for his ability to forthrightly name the *enemy* (and to recognize that the West continues to confront deadly enemies) in a democratic world that is increasingly prone to take for granted the spiritual unity of the human race. But this admirable clarity about the moral dimensions of the struggle also leads the president to be too dismissive of the gray middle ground that more often than not defines the art of statecraft. Bush and his neoconservative allies paradoxically share no small measure of the humanitarianism that they rightly castigate when it emanates from antipolitical European and American leftist intellectuals.

It should be acknowledged that the Bush administration's instincts and policies are often significantly more prudent than its official rhetoric and doctrine suggest. The administration has no doubt been chastened by the difficulty of pacifying Iraq and of introducing lawful government in a country wracked by tribal passions and sectarian divisions. Through bitter experience, it has come to appreciate the profound difficulties entailed in bringing self-government to another people, especially one that has been deeply scarred by despotism and is bereft of a settled national consciousness. The administration surely has arrived at a more sober appreciation of the sheer intractability of a part of the world deeply rooted in spiritual sources that are alien to the

Western experience. Contrary to what its more fevered critics suggest, it has no stomach for organizing a global democratic imperium or embarking on new "wars of choice." While the administration continues to put too much emphasis on the centrality of electoral democracy, it knows how to work with "authoritarian" allies who oppose Islamist fanaticism or who, in its judgment, provide the best hope for political stability and gradual liberalization.

Conservatism and the Rhetoric of Democracy

But the administration's official rhetoric continues to be marred by a tendency to treat modern democracy as a self-evident desideratum, even as the regime "according to nature." As friendly critics such as Fareed Zakaria have pointed out, both the administration and its neoconservative allies woefully underestimate the despotic propensities inherent in electoral democracy, and this despite the rising electoral fortunes of Islamist parties such as the Muslim Brotherhood and Hamas in the Middle East and of a leftist authoritarian like Hugo Chavez in Latin America. They continue to speak ritualistically about "democracy" when what they must really have in mind is that complex synthesis of the rule of law, constitutionalism, federalism, and representative government that Zakaria calls "constitutional liberalism." Their "democratic" monomania marks a break with an older conservative tradition which always insisted that Western liberty draws on intellectual and spiritual resources broader and deeper than that of modern democracy. The idioms of constitutionalism and representative government have little room in a doctrine that places such inordinate emphasis on the love of liberty in the human soul and its natural expression through majority votes.

Critics who raise perfectly legitimate and necessary questions about the cultural prerequisites of democratic self-government are summarily dismissed by President Bush or Prime Minister Blair as cultural relativists, or even as racists—as if "democracy" arises automatically once impediments are removed. Just as ominously, the partisans of "global democracy" turn a blind eye to the historical evidence that suggests it is not from authoritarian regimes, but from weak and fledgling "democracies," that totalitarianism arises: consider Russia in 1917, Italy in 1922, and Germany in 1933.[3] The best conservative thinkers of the last two centuries have been wary of unalloyed democracy precisely because they cared deeply about the preservation of human liberty and recognized the powerful affinities between mass democracy and modern totalitarianism. There are totalitarian propensities inherent in what the French political philosopher Bertrand de Jouvenel once called "sovereignty in itself": the illusion that the "sovereign" human will is the ultimate arbiter of the moral and political world.

Daniel J. Mahoney

We are confronted, then, with a foreign policy that in many respects operates within sober parameters of principle and prudence—but which is expressed in a self-defeating rhetoric that both encourages overreach and leaves the administration vulnerable to tendentious criticism. When the administration works with moderate pro-American autocrats such as General Pervez Musharraf in Pakistan it is inevitably accused of hypocrisy. Putting inordinate stress on the necessity of building *democracy* in Iraq and Afghanistan—rather than speaking more modestly about strengthening lawful and representative institutions in both countries—creates unreasonable expectations that are bound to be disappointed. Such "democracy" rhetoric also disarms the United States' legitimate concerns about religious extremism (e.g., the imposition of *Sharia*) when it is legitimized through the electoral process. Who are we to challenge the sovereignty of a *democratic* people? A more calibrated rhetoric, one that emphasizes the need to gradually introduce lawful and nondespotic political orders in countries ravaged by despotism or beset by corruption and authoritarianism, would be less dramatic and perhaps less inspiring. But it would better describe the more modest and often quite realistic hopes that drive *actual* American policy in countries such as Iraq and Afghanistan.

Excessively doctrinaire rhetoric about democracy also creates misplaced pressures to confront nontotalitarian regimes, such as Vladimir Putin's Russia, with demands for "liberalization" that have nothing to do with America's legitimate national interests and everything to do with the view that Western-style liberal democracy provides the only legitimate model for political development in our time. This necessarily puts the administration in binds. The vice president of the United States followed up a May 4, 2006, speech in Vilnius, Lithuania—one which implicitly threatened Russia with a "color revolution" of its own if it did not move in a more "democratic" direction—with trips to Kazakhstan and Khirgistan to do business with the local tyrants. Such a brazen act of double-dealing confirms the suspicions of skeptics who are already convinced that American "universalism" is little more than a cover for national egoism and will-to-power. The spirited resistance to tyranny that has been the hallmark of administration rhetoric since 9/11 needs to be moderated and complemented by a greater awareness of local conditions and a greater modesty about America's capacity to judge—and dictate—the appropriate conditions for self-government abroad. In Russia, "National Bolsheviks" of the most unsavory sort, not Western-style liberals, are the real alternative to Putin's comparatively liberal regime.

And in truth, the vituperative exchanges between neoconservatives and paleoconservatives, and between foreign policy "realists" and "idealists," do little to contribute to the articulation of a politics of prudence worthy of the name. Both the administration and the full array of American conservative intellectuals need to learn how to judiciously combine spiritedness and moderation, Churchillian fortitude and prudent self-restraint, in a way that does justice to the perils that stem from both too much and too little national self-assertion.

The Second Inaugural: Nature, History, and the Human Soul

The democratic universalism of the Bush Doctrine is expressed with particular lucidity in the Second Inaugural Address delivered by the president on January 21, 2005. That speech is the best single articulation of the moral and philosophical premises underlying contemporary American foreign policy—or at least of the official doctrine that animates it. But it also reveals some of the deeply problematic assumptions informing the administration's policy "to seek and support the growth of democratic movements and institutions in every nation and culture, with the ultimate goal of ending tyranny in our world." That heady goal is presented as a fully practical ideal, even if Bush conceded on that occasion that it is likely to be the "concentrated work of generations." That perfunctory concession to gradualism in no way qualifies the president's "complete confidence in the eventual triumph of freedom" or his belief that democracy, and democracy alone, is the regime that most fully coheres with the nature and needs of human beings. For President Bush, democracy has the support of the deepest longings of the human soul and of a providential God who is also the "Author of Liberty."

To be sure, President Bush acknowledges that democracy can take a variety of local or cultural expressions. He denies that the United States has any interest in "impos(ing) our own style of government on the unwilling." Still, he fully identifies democracy as a political form with the imperative of self-government. Whatever latitude is left to citizens and statesmen has to do with the *kind of democracy* that will protect human rights and human dignity within particular historical or cultural settings. President Bush implicitly affirms that the whole of humanity should and will eventually live under the liberal democratic dispensation. To that extent at least, he shares the Kojèvean-Fukuyaman premise that the "mutual recognition" of man by man will inevitably culminate in a "universal and homogenous state."

In the Second Inaugural, Bush speaks grandiloquently about "the global appeal of liberty" and makes no distinction between support for liberty and the promotion of a rather ill-defined "democracy." The president simply ignores or disregards everything in modern historical experience that suggests that modernization is compatible with various forms of "democratic despotism." The defeat of communism is interpreted as definitive proof that "the world is moving toward liberty," since "the call of freedom comes to every mind and every soul."

Daniel J. Mahoney

In his quite complimentary remarks to the people of Hungary delivered on June 22, 2006, in commemoration of the fiftieth anniversary of the Hungarian Revolution, President Bush makes a similar claim that "the desire for liberty is universal, because it is written by our Creator into the hearts of every man, woman, and child on the Earth." In this speech, Bush pays eloquent tribute to the noble struggle of Hungarians in 1956, all the while treating that "anti-totalitarian revolution" (as Raymond Aron called it at the time), that collective revolt against the ideological "lie," as evidence of the inevitable triumph of democracy over "dictatorship." In doing so, however, he risks rendering that great event banal by turning it into one more illustration of the "Whig" version of history. The specificity of communist totalitarianism, the Christian and European character of the Hungarian people, and the fact that Hungarians themselves took the initiative to restore their national independence and the authentic meaning of words are all overlooked in this rendering of events. The Hungarian Revolution instead becomes raw material for the inevitable victory of democracy in every time and place.

As hortatory rhetoric, the president's words are undoubtedly stirring and even ennobling. As political reflection, they reveal a shallow understanding of the complex passions, interests, and motives that move human beings. President Bush dogmatically presupposes that love of liberty is the predominant, even the overarching motive of the human soul. He not only downplays the cultural prerequisites of ordered liberty or democratic self-government but abstracts from the sempiternal drama of good and evil in each and every human soul. The president's unqualified universalism abstracts from the fact that hatred of despotism by no means automatically translates into love of liberty or a settled and disciplined capacity for self-government. It ignores Tocqueville's profound insight that the pure love of liberty—the passion for political freedom and of "government of God and the laws alone"—is a "sublime taste" reserved for a few souls and incomprehensible to "mediocre" ones.[4]

To be sure, Bush sometimes recurs to the best conservative wisdom and acknowledges that self-government necessarily entails "the governing of the self." He rightly asserts that human rights are "ennobled by service, and mercy." But he more characteristically makes extravagant claims about love of liberty being the incontestable motive of thinking and acting man. As Charles Kesler has observed, Bush ignores the palpable fact that while "'people everywhere prefer freedom to slavery' . . . many people everywhere and at all times have been quite happy to enjoy their freedom and all the benefits of someone else's slavery."[5] Self-government is a disposition of the soul that finds powerful support in the soul's refusal to be tyrannized by others. But the two are not equivalent. President Bush is not wrong when he argues that despotism violates the moral law and mutilates the wellsprings of the human spirit. But he is too quick to identify human nature with a single overarching impulse or desire, and he goes too far in conflating the ways of Providence with the empire of human liberty.

Near the end of the Second Inaugural, Bush anticipates some of these criticisms. While continuing to express "complete confidence in the eventual triumph of freedom" he attempts to distance himself from arguments about historical inevitability. "History" by itself determines nothing. Instead, our confidence in the universal triumph of liberty must be rooted in the fact that freedom is the "permanent hope of mankind" and the most powerful "longing of the soul." These poetic invocations do not adequately take into account the decidedly "mixed" character of human nature. The president should not be expected, of course, to speak with the precision of a political philosopher. Still, this president of deep Christian conviction paradoxically shows little appreciation for the tragic dimensions of history and the pernicious and permanent effects of original sin on individual and collective life.

Humanitarian Democracy versus the United States

Moreover, the reduction of the political problem to the categorical imperative of promoting democracy abroad leaves the administration and the country vulnerable to those on the left who identify democracy with a project to emancipate human beings from traditional cultural, moral, and even political restraints. For the partisans of "postmodern" or "humanitarian" democracy, the United States falls far short of the "democratic ideal." As the French political philosopher Pierre Manent has recently written, European elites "are trying to separate their democratic virtue from all their other characteristics," such as tradition, religion, and especially from the political framework of the nation-state. They have succumbed to what might be called the "postpolitical temptation." At the same time, "Americans seem more than ever willing—and this disposition extends well beyond the partisans of the current administration—to *identify* everything they do and everything they are with democracy, as such."[6] But what is to prevent the partisans of humanitarian democracy from denying the democratic *bona fides* of a self-governing people that remains attached to national sovereignty and still acknowledges the importance of traditional arrangements to a regime of self-government? By validating democracy as the *alpha* and *omega* of politics in our time, the Bush Doctrine leaves America vulnerable to delegitimization at the hands of more radical and "consistent" forms of democratic affirmation. In any case, deference to humanizing universal moral and political truths in no way means that any particular country gives humanity unmediated access to the universal. Abraham Lincoln, the noble poet-statesman of the American experiment, beautifully captured this tension when he spoke of the United States as an "almost chosen nation." America (and the Western world in general) would cease to be true to itself if it repudiated the universality of its principles. But America surely also owes much of its greatness to particular national characteristics, to what Orestes Brownson has suggestively called our "providential constitution." Otherwise America is in principle "the world," the prototype of a unified humanity, and is destined to be swallowed up by a global imperium that more fully embodies the "democratic" aspirations of the whole of mankind.

President Bush may not be a neoconservative in any narrow political or even ideological sense. But his Second Inaugural Address perfectly mirrors the contradictions at the heart of the second neoconservatism. Like President Bush, neoconservatives are proud defenders of the prerogatives of the United States as a free, independent, and self-governing national community. At the same time, they are deeply suspicious of any other national self-assertion, however moderate or humane, that declines to "identify American democracy with the universal as such."[7] At the rhetorical level at least, the second neoconservatism and the partisans of European humanitarian democracy ultimately differ more about means than ends. They are "frères-ennemis" who promote two distinct paths to the same destination, the "universal and homogenous state."

As I have tried to suggest, neoconservatism's misplaced one-sided emphasis on democracy may be more the rhetorical scaffolding than the heart and soul of neoconservative wisdom. But this democratic monomania acts as an acid, eating away at the coherence of a current of thought whose patriotism, good will, and commitment to the cause of liberty should in no way be doubted. Alas, it cannot provide the basis for a politics of prudence in our time.

7

Add, Don't Subtract:
How Christian Conservatives Should
Engage American Culture

Marvin Olasky

RONALD REAGAN AWAKENED AMERICA. He ran on a platform that emphasized standing up to communism abroad and high-taxers domestically. The Bible tells us—eight times in Deuteronomy, Joshua, and 1st and 2nd Chronicles alone—to "be strong and courageous," and President Reagan was. Using a coalition of conservatives and libertarians he fought both double-digit inflation and Soviet expansionism, and when he left office both bears were tamed. Soon, Republicans gained a majority in the House of Representatives for the first time in forty years.

In 2006 the parties remain differentiated on foreign policy and abortion, but in other areas—government spending and corruption—Republicans are doing no better than the Democrats of 1994. Many have ignored the small-government principles that brought Ronald Reagan and themselves to office. Arrogance and Abramoff crouch at every Washington door, and it's easy for those in power to think that they'll use it for purposes of righteousness or riches. Either way, government stays big, and libertarians as well as most conservatives are frustrated. The coalition that Ronald Reagan put together is close to a crack-up.

The future of American conservatism depends on the ability of libertarians to understand that liberty without virtue cannot last, and the ability of Christian conservatives to understand that being strong and courageous does not mean demanding ideological purity. Both parts of the coalition need to follow the Reagan practice of reasoning politely and patiently with those who disagree, giving in on secondary matters, and searching for common ground. Both parts of the coalition may need to sacrifice a little.

This chapter concentrates on what Christian conservatives should do. It first lays out a basic biblical exegesis that frees Christians from reacting defensively, and provides examples of how our goal should be to add, not subtract. It then explores some of the nuances, including: why America is not the new Israel, why theocracy is not biblically warranted here, what the minimal societal goals for Christians should be, how Christians can steer clear of spam evangelism, how the difficult issue of same-sex marriage should be approached, and how Christ's expansive definition of "neighbor" fits well with the Constitution's first three words: "We, the people."

Basics for Believers

My oversimplified advice to American Christian conservatives: Be New Testament, not Old Testament. By this I don't mean that the two parts of revelation are theologically distinct, for as the couplet sums it up, "The New is in the Old contained, the Old is by the New explained." I am suggesting that the emphasis is different: to generalize enormously, the Old concentrates on subtracting, the New on adding, and the success of the American experiment has hinged on our willingness to add.

The Old Testament emphasizes subtracting a family and then a nation (and its land) from the idol-worship that surrounded first Abraham and then Israel. The emphasis was on purity, not evangelism, so God sent Ishmael and Esau out of the land, told Joshua to destroy the Canaanites, and instructed Ezra to insist that the Israelites put away foreign wives. To make the Holy Land holy, God commanded a zero-tolerance policy: No abominations among you. Nothing. Nada.

The Holy Land was man's greatest opportunity to set up a new kind of Eden. It wasn't the Eden at the beginning of Genesis, because sin still burdened man, the earth yielded its produce reluctantly, and earthly life still ended in death. But it was a semi-Eden—a land flowing in milk and honey—and it had God's semi-presence as He facilitated prophecy and gave specific advice via the casting of lots and the mysterious Urim and Thummim. God chose a particular nation to live in his semi-Eden, provided commandments so they knew what to do day by day, inspired a history so they knew where they came from, and promised them that if they obeyed all would go well.

This holy land, this semi-Eden, was supposed to be spotless, a serious equivalent of Disneyland in which not a single candy wrapper is to stay on the ground for even a few minutes. Sadly, God's model country, like the Model

Cities of the 1960s, turned out to be a model for despair. The great tragedy of ancient Israel was that God's chosen people sinned in a land that of all lands should have been the least conducive to sin. The great lesson is that sin comes from within all of us, not from our surroundings. God was teaching that sin crouches at our door even in the best of environments, whether the original Eden or Israel's semi-Eden. He was teaching man's desperate need for Christ: accept no substitutes!

As early Christians came to understand the meaning of Israel's history, they were ready to understand the New Testament emphasis on adding. The Jewish answer to the question "Who is my neighbor?" was often "your fellow Jew," and sometimes just the Jews who lived close by. Jesus added to that understanding by eating with tax collectors and others seen as sinners, by stating that anyone in need is our neighbor, and by adding women, Samaritans, and even enemy soldiers to the list of God's people.

Instructed to take the gospel to all nations and not concentrate on defending one, Christians were free to evangelize and admit to church membership anyone who confessed faith in Christ, regardless of pedigree, past sins, race, or ethnicity. Would some get in who should not, and as a result would the visible church display visible sin? Absolutely, but a Christian understanding of the omnipresence of sin makes even the best screen about as effective as bed nets against malarial mosquitoes in Africa: the mosquitoes will find a way to get in.

Christian conservatives need to apply such thinking to our political processes. In discussing American conservatism a football metaphor seems appropriate: Better to win the game 35–14 than to emphasize the avoidance of mistakes so that the best we can hope for is a 3–3 tie. Instead of fearfully assuming that nothing will get done unless the federal government does it, and rushing to increase spending whenever a problem arises, we can renew Ronald Reagan's small-government coalition by adding to our societal list of problem-solvers the civic and religious groups that often do a better job than government.

We should be willing to work in a political coalition with a wide variety of non-Christians, because our goal should not be to subtract "the impure" by differentiating ourselves from coalition members who don't share our theology or our particular political strategy. We ourselves are impure, after all. Rather, our goal should be to add new opportunities by enlisting all those who agree with us on some issues, even if they disagree on others. I'll offer three examples—one cultural, one symbolic, and one that's life-and-death—of how Christian conservatives should add rather than subtract.

The first concerns our culture wars. Year after year Christians have called for boycotts of this or that art exhibition, movie, or television show. For example, in 1999 Christian groups wanted government funding removed from a profane show at the Brooklyn Museum of Art that featured a dung-displaying portrait of the Virgin Mary. The protest led to front-page stories about Christians trying to keep people from viewing art, and to record attendance at the exhibit. It would have been far better to push for a parallel show displaying the work of Christian artists. In 2004 and 2005 we had such parallel shows in the movie theaters: Mel Gibson's *The Passion of the Christ* (which reaped a rich bonanza in evangelism and ticket sales) and *The Lion, the Witch, and the Wardrobe*. Both Christian conservatives and libertarians could salute these examples of adding.

For a way to deal with symbolic issues, compare Judge Roy Moore's plopping down a two-and-a-half-ton block of granite in the rotunda of the Alabama Judicial Building to Texas Attorney General Greg Abbott's defense before the U.S. Supreme Court of a six-foot-tall red granite monolith located about seventy-five feet from the Texas state capitol building in Austin. Moore's in-your-face Ten Commandments monument gesture gained whoops of support from some Christians but hisses from libertarians, and of course an aggressive response from federal courts. But Abbott, also a Christian, gained broad support by pointing out that a representation of Aztec mythology was already in the state capitol, and just as he had no problem with that, others should not have a problem with a Judeo-Christian monument. The U.S. Supreme Court and conservatives of many stripes agreed with his "add, don't subtract" thinking.

My last example is the life-and-death matter. Christian conservatives would like to see a constitutional amendment adding protection for human life, but neither culturally nor politically are we there yet, since journalists and many others depict pro-life activities as subtracting freedom. We can save lives and also build support by adding options for women surprised by pregnancy. Instead of asking them to choose between abortion and single parenting—which to many women seems a choice between legal homicide and life imprisonment—we can save lives by making real a third choice, adoption, and not overlooking the possibility of a fourth, marriage. We can add soul-stirring information to the decision process by using ultrasound machines to show the baby who could be killed. We can add other people to the decision process by requiring that the pregnant woman's parents and the unborn child's father be informed.

Few of my recommended actions would be sufficient for those who demand an Old Testament defense of America as the new holy land, but they're consistent with the New Testament approach practiced by Paul and others in mixed cultures from Rome to the present: Instead of working fruitlessly to subtract evil from the land, add the good. American conservatism can have a bright future, with God's grace, if we are strong and courageous in developing positive alternatives to the cultural negativities around us. But if we merely praise our own Christian circles and curse the darkness outside them, we will soon be surrounded by it.

This type of guerrilla cultural warfare can be more difficult than an invasion of Canaan—but God calls Christians to help transform the societies surrounding them. In the history books of the Old Testament "Be strong and courageous" clearly had a military edge. Yet by New Testament times, when the early Christians were in a culture war without clear front lines, the apostle Paul was telling the Corinthians, living in one of the empire's most dissolute cities, "Be strong. Let all that you do be done in love" (I Corinthians 16:13).

Strength and love—we rarely see them put together in that way, but Paul did so appropriately because he was teaching people to walk in Christ's steps. Certainly no one was stronger than Jesus: His strength was so great that he did not sin, unlike everyone else in history. But this strong man was gentle with ordinary people, seeing them as sheep without a shepherd. He was particularly gentle with those outside of Israel, like the Samaritan woman (John 4) and the Syro-Phoenician woman (Mark 7).

Certainly, Jesus was harsh to the ostentatiously religious: "You Pharisees cleanse the outside of the cup and of the dish, but inside you are full of greed and wickedness." Certainly, he criticized those who invented laws beyond those demanded by the Bible: "You load people with burdens hard to bear, and you yourselves do not touch the burdens with one of your fingers" (Luke 11:39, 46). But his most famous speech, the Sermon on the Mount, is far from Joshua's commanded violence, and far even from the style of violent prophetic speech that we call jeremiads. Christ was calm rather than clamorous, beckoning rather than beheading.

Christians should walk in Christ's steps and mirror his tone in talking with those heading in the wrong direction. That's the big picture. But having shown that, I'd like to offer not ten commandments but ten thoughts about nuances, starting with one that further explains the Old Testament/New Testament difference.

Nuance 1:
The Importance of Location

The Old Testament is highly location-specific. For example, when God teaches Israelites in the wilderness how they should behave in the Promised Land, He says plainly, "you shall not do as they do in the land of Canaan, to which I am bringing you." He then provides a long list of what the Canaanites do and what His people should not do, and specifies (Leviticus 18:26, 28) that "You shall keep my statutes and my rules and do none of these abominations, either the native or the stranger who sojourns among you . . . lest the land vomit you out when you make it unclean. . . ."

This emphasis on not only pure people but a pure country is frequent in Old Testament passages about life in Israel. Deuteronomy 18:9 is typical: "When you come into the land that the Lord your God is giving you, you shall not learn to follow the abominable practices of those nations. There shall not be found among you anyone" who does these things. Note well: We learn throughout the Bible that God's people themselves should not follow these practices at any time, but the emphasis here is on when "you come into the land." The land must be cleansed from defilement. It must be preserved as holy.

Penalties for disobedience in the land were severe, as noted in Leviticus 20: 10,13: "If a man commits adultery with the wife of his neighbor, both the adulterer and the adulteress shall surely be put to death. . . . If a man lies with a male as with a woman, both of them have committed an abomination; they shall surely be put to death. . . ." OBEY, God shouted, so "that the land where I am bringing you to live may not vomit you out" (Leviticus 20:22). God established many specific practices for that land: familial property cannot be sold permanently; certain cities of refuge must be established; on it goes.

The prophets were indignant when the Israelites trashed their semi-Eden. God had Jeremiah proclaim, "Thus says the Lord . . . 'I brought you into a plentiful land to enjoy its fruits and its good things. But when you came in, you defiled my land and made my heritage an abomination" (Jeremiah 2:7). Jeremiah denounced the betrayal: "The Lord once called you 'a green olive tree, beautiful with good fruit.' But with the roar of a great tempest He will set fire to it, and its branches will be consumed" (Jeremiah 11:16).

The charter of the ancient Israelites was to protect the purity of the land God had given them. Evangelism was not a priority; when some Israelites married foreign women, leaders from Moses to Ezra did not look upon this as an opportunity to evangelize the newcomers and increase the numbers of Israel, but instead looked upon intermarriage with horror. The Israelites were to purify the Holy Land by killing or driving out the nations that inhabited it and surrounding their land with a theological and cultural fence to keep out others. *The prime directive was defense, with the maintenance of holiness as the goal.*

Most Christians understand that Old Testament history teaches all of us not to become full of ourselves and think we can create earthly utopias or even sustain the ones handed to us. But other questions also arise from Israel's experience: If ancient Israel's laws, given by God, did not bring about righteousness in this most likely of environments, how likely are holiness laws to succeed in less favorable environments? And should those who want to be strong and courageous strive to make whatever country they inhabit the semi-Eden that ancient Israel was to be?

Marvin Olasky

Nuance 2:
Examining the "New Israel" View

The records of New Haven, Connecticut, in the 1640s show this decision: "It was ordered that the judicial laws of God, as they were delivered by Moses . . . be a rule to all the courts in this jurisdiction in their proceedings against offenders." From the Puritans to the present, some Christians who view America as the new Israel have been unwilling to accept unholy activities on what they see as holy ground.

To take one twentieth-century example, the idea that it was sacrilegious in America to have anti-biblical doctrines taught in government-funded schools was part of the thinking of many Tennessee legislators in the 1920s when they forbad public school teachers to teach "that man has descended from a lower order of animals." John Butler, the legislator who introduced the anti-evolution bill, told reporters, "I am not opposed to teaching of evolution, but I don't think it ought to be taught in state-supported schools." If an anti-biblical doctrine were given governmental backing, this holy land would be profaned.

The debate over the Ten Commandments monument in Alabama also showed the potency of the new-Israel view. Former Alabama Chief Justice Roy Moore wrote in his autobiography *So Help Me God* that "our country is being led to deny the existence of the Creator God. This turning away from God is known as apostasy and, unfortunately, is nothing new." He then described the situation in ancient Israel, and particularly remarked upon the situation of the southern kingdom, Judah: "Like America today, Judah was a nation that called upon God's name but refused to recognize his sovereignty or abide by his law."

Throughout his jeremiad, Judge Moore treated America as the new Israel and mourned its departure from biblical ways. His supporters similarly argued that court-ordered removal of the monument was blasphemy. Before the dirty deed, Rev. Greg Dixon of Indiana said, "To remove those commandments would be to replace them with men's commandments that would elevate man to godhood which would replace the divine Godhead, Father, Son, and Holy Ghost." Afterward, Covenantnews.com cited chapter five of Deuteronomy, where Moses recites commandments listed in Exodus and then states, "You shall write them on the doorposts of your house and upon your gates." Since "the word 'gates' of Deuteronomy 6:9 refers to public places," Covenantnews.com declared that the monument must be displayed.

That website, like many others, took a question about which Christians can disagree and transformed it into a test of faith. Those who did not back Moore suddenly were heretics. Seeing America as the new Israel, though, was wrong both in principle (biblically, the Church—not any particular nation—is the new Israel) and practice. Practically, the battle for granite gave media a terrific opportunity to further the sense among scoffers that Christianity is primarily about cold do's and don'ts rather than about a warm-hearted relationship with God.

Predictably biased coverage of monument defenders advanced the media stereotypes of Christians demanding political victory rather than showing forbearance. More people began or continued to see Christianity as a power-seeking faith rather than one emphasizing grace. If the chief Christian goal is the defense of America against the defilement produced by the absence of governmental recognition that God is sovereign, then Judge Moore fought for a noble cause, regardless of the predictability of defeat. But if evangelism is central, then the monument contretemps was for Christians a self-inflicted wound.

Non-Christians now typically believe that Christianity takes away freedom rather than adds to it. Two weeks after Judge Moore's stand hit the headlines I asked students in my University of Texas course on journalism and religion to give top-of-the-head, anonymous responses to this question: "How do Christians act?" Here were typical answers: "Fanatical. Cram religion down others' throats. Want to push their religion on others. Trying to force others to do everything their way. Bossing, not helping, others."

Nuance 3:
How the New-Israel View Plays Out Across the Country

Judge Moore received national attention, but many localities sport small groups with views similar to his. For example, Michael Marcavage, leader of the Philadelphia-area "Repent America," trumpeted on his website that organization's success in reclaiming at one demonstration a piece of pavement that gay activists had seized: "As soon as we arrived at the protest, I placed my wooden chair in the medium strip facing the protesters. Then, I stood upon the chair and held the Christian flag high. Almost immediately, the crowd across the street turned, surrounded me, and began chanting and taking pictures."

It seems unlikely that they were taking pictures to illustrate a book on effective techniques of evangelism. When I interviewed him in 2005 Marcavage stated that he considered it his duty to reclaim those several square feet for Christ, since America should be a holy land as Israel was. Every October he and several of his supporters march through "OutFest," a gay pride event that sprawls over many city blocks in downtown Philadelphia, carrying signs that say "God Abhors You" and reciting imprecatory psalms through a bullhorn.

Marcavage now has a long record of arrests for demonstration-related charges such as disorderly conduct, and one year he added felony charges for allegedly trying to start a riot and disobeying the police. The felony charges were clearly overwrought, and even the liberal *Philadelphia Inquirer* said so, so it was good and right that the charges eventually were dismissed. But the *Inquirer* correctly scolded the protesters for refusing to obey police orders to take their bullhorns and signs to the periphery of the demonstration.

Should Marcavage let gays have their day in the fall sun without the benefit of Repent America's bullhorn? Many Christians not known for wimping out publicly criticized Marcavage's approach. The Rev. Peter Lillback, pastor of Proclamation Presbyterian Church in Bryn Mawr and a radio evangelist, stated that "drowning people out with a bullhorn is inappropriate." The Rev. Herb Lusk, pastor of Greater Exodus Baptist Church and an ex-NFL tailback who preached regularly to the prostitutes who used to close deals on his doorstep, said biblical opposition to homosexuality "should be preached without apology, [but] that preaching has to be coupled with love and compassion or there's a problem with it."

Bill Devlin of the Urban Family Council and Calvary Chapel called Marcavage's tactics "a classic case of the messenger getting in the way of the message," and that is the critical insight. Marcavage's work was counter-productive: gays who need Christ, as all of us do, are now more likely to associate Christianity with a bullhorn than with compassion. Marcavage's behavior emerged not from bad manners but bad theology. By identifying America with ancient Israel and himself with Jeremiah, Marcavage's response went this way: "This is what we should expect from the world. They killed all the prophets."

Well, yes and no: ancient Israelites did kill prophets, but some prophets outside of Israel—such as Jonah and Daniel—survived through God's grace and even succeeded: the kings of Assyria and Babylonia listened to them. One problem with expectations such as Marcavage's is that they can be self-fulfilling prophecies, leading Christians to think they are failures unless others consider them repulsive.

Nuance 4:
Living Outside Israel in Ancient Times

When we examine several Old Testament books that deal with the situation of God's people living outside God's model country, the basic Old Testament/ New Testament, subtracting-vs.-adding distinction holds, but the division becomes more complex. Significantly, Jeremiah—the same Jeremiah whose godly fury led to our word "jeremiads"—had a very different tone when he spoke to Israelites living not only outside the semi-Eden but in the anti-Eden, Babylonia.

Look at what Jeremiah wrote to Israelites living in the capital of that very ungodly country: "This is what the LORD Almighty, the God of Israel, says to all those I carried into exile from Jerusalem to Babylon: 'Build houses and live in them; plant gardens and eat their produce. . . . Seek the welfare of the city where I have sent you into exile, and pray to the LORD on its behalf, because in its welfare you will find your welfare'" (Jeremiah 29:4–7).

Other parts of the Old Testament also indicate that Israelites outside the borders of Israel could have a different political agenda than those inside. Deuteronomy 18:9 banned from ancient Israel "anyone who practices divination or tells fortunes or interprets omens, or a sorcerer or a charmer or a medium or a wizard or a necromancer, for whoever does such things is an abomination to the Lord." And yet the Book of Daniel shows how Daniel had to hang out with enchanters, sorcerers, and the other wise men of Babylon. Daniel thought and acted independently, but he nowhere indicated a plan or desire to wipe out these ungodly people. A stranger in a strange land, he had to coexist with them.

The Books of Ezra, Nehemiah, and Esther show how the Jews of Persia, part of an empire comprising 127 provinces and a vast number of ethnic groups and languages, also lived under laws not their own. The evil that God had said Israel must ban was often just around the corner in Persia, but Israelites showed themselves to be often the most patriotic of subjects: Cupbearer Nehemiah was the last defense against attempts to poison the king, and Mordecai in the book of Esther broke up an assassination plot. When Esther and her uncle Mordecai later had an opportunity to have the king promulgate legislation, they only requested that the Jews of Persia have the right to fight back militarily against their persecutors.

Worth noting is that none of the Israelites' public tolerance of differences indicated a failure to keep God's commands in their own lives and within their own households. In chapter three of the Book of Daniel, King Nebuchadnezzar sets up a ninety-foot-tall image of gold and commands all his officials to bow down and worship it. Three Israelite refuseniks do not stand on a chair in front of it and harangue the assembled pagans; they merely do not show up. In chapter six, when King Darius orders that for thirty days all prayers must be addressed to him, Daniel prays in his own home, as he always did, until his enemies spy on him and arrest him. Biblical heroes typically did not go looking for trouble. Trouble went looking for them.

Nuance 5:
More about Location

It might be said that these societies had no tradition of free speech and public demonstration, so there is limited relevance in the Bible commanding a very hard line within ancient Israel as opposed to a "Why can't we all get along?" posture elsewhere. But in New Testament times when limited liberty did exist for Roman citizens (but not others) in some parts of the empire, the apostle Paul and others emphasized proclaiming the gospel at every opportunity, without suggesting that the imposition of biblical law was their desired outcome.

Gideon in Israel had destroyed an altar of Baal (Judges 6). About a thousand years later the Maccabees had destroyed Greek altars erected in Israel. Paul, though, did not damage the numerous altars he saw during his walk through Athens. Instead, he reasoned "in the marketplace every day with those who happened to be there" and also spoke before the city's philosophical elite (Acts 17). Paul never hesitated to demand his rights as a Roman citizen, but he also never tried to subtract from city streets pagan altars and idols. Proper action in one place was not proper in another.

The bottom line: location, location, location. We even see this in the work of Jesus: He drove the moneychangers out of the Temple, the holiest place in the world, but did not drive them out of other places. Israel had already become a most unholy land by AD 70, when Roman soldiers destroyed the Temple, and after that there was no reason to consider one land holier than another, and to institute outside of Israel what was made for Israel.

The early Christian church dropped the defensive posture that had characterized Israel and went on offense. Without a land to preserve but with a gospel to proclaim, the prime directive was evangelism rather than maintenance of purity. New people rapidly joined the church at the risk of dilution, but leaders impelled by the Great Commission of proclaiming the gospel in all nations took risks that Jewish leaders directed to maintain purity were never willing to accept.

Nuance 6:
Three Types of Biblical Law

Now, let's move to America and theological writings essential to the Founding. I've written elsewhere that an alliance of Christian conservatives and libertarians led to the successful prosecution of the Revolutionary War and adoption of the Constitution.[1] If Christian conservatives then had been determined to impose a theonomic structure on the new United States, the result would have been continued disunity. Christians had flexibility, though, because they had grown up on the two theological works that (besides the Bible) were the most influential in colonial America, John Calvin's *Institutes of the Christian Religion* (1536-64) and the *Westminster Confession of Faith* (1644-46).

Some portray Calvin as a theonomist, but he emphasized the lessons of the biblical books I've cited and noted in his blunt fashion (book 4, chapter 20, section 14), "There are some who deny that a commonwealth is duly framed which neglects the political system of Moses, and is ruled by the common laws of nations." He called such a view "perilous and seditious . . . false and foolish," and proposed instead a classic tripartite formulation in his heading for section 15: "Moral, ceremonial, and judicial law distinguished."

The moral law, Calvin wrote, is "contained under two heads, one of which simply commands us to worship God with pure faith and piety; the other, to embrace men with sincere affection. Accordingly, it is the true and eternal rule of righteousness, prescribed for men of all nations and times, who wish to conform their lives to God's will." Or, to translate into the words of the movie Casablanca, "A kiss is still a kiss . . . the fundamental things apply, as times goes by." (Christians should be fundamentalists of that sort.)

After toasting the moral law, Calvin roasted the ceremonial law, made up of those sections of the Bible dealing with sacrifices and Temple worship: "The ceremonial law was the tutelage of the Jews, with which it seemed good to the Lord to train this people, as it were, in their childhood, until the fullness of time should come." He quoted Paul's explanation (Galatians 3:23) that "the law was our guardian until Christ came"—but since then, Christ's sacrifice has rendered all other sacrifices unnecessary and thus disrespectful of God.

The hard question then and now concerned the third kind of law, that known to the ancient Israelites and defined by Calvin as "the judicial law, given to them for civil government." He opposed the idea that the legal code of ancient Israel should be transplanted into different societies: "The statement of some, that the law of God given through Moses is dishonored when it is abrogated and new laws preferred to *it,* is utterly vain." Legislators should pay attention to "times, place, and nation. . . . For the Lord through the hand of Moses did not give that law to be proclaimed among all nations and to be in force everywhere." In other words, location, location, location.

Since God did give Israel its judicial law, we can learn from the equity of that law—the principles of justice that it embodies. But equity, Calvin emphasized, "cannot but be the same for all. . . . Constitutions have certain circumstances upon which they in part depend. It therefore does not matter that they are different, provided all equally press toward the same goal of equity. . . . Whatever laws shall be framed to that rule, directed to that goal, bound by that limit, there is no reason why we should disapprove of them, howsoever they may differ from the Jewish law, or among themselves." The stereotype of Calvin has him as doctrinaire and unbending, but in this area and many others he wanted flexibility.

A century later, the *Westminster Confession of Faith* framed Calvin's argument in a way that proved highly influential in the United States, particularly through the influence of the Presbyterian Church. *Westminster* noted the Bible's basic ethical principles and continued: "Beside this law, commonly called moral, God was pleased to give to the people of Israel, as a church under age, ceremonial laws, containing several typical ordinances, partly of worship, prefiguring Christ, his graces, actions, sufferings, and benefits; and partly, holding forth divers instructions of moral duties. All which ceremonial laws are now abrogated, under the new testament."

Here's the crucial passage: God also gave Israel "sundry judicial laws, which expired together with the State of that people; not obliging any other now, further than the general equity thereof may require." Or, as Rev. Ligon Duncan, moderator of the 2004 general assembly of the Presbyterian Church in America (theological successor to the Westminster divines) put it, the judicial code "was given in a unique situation, under temporary circumstances, to a particular people, serving in a special capacity. Thus when the nation-state of Israel expired, its civil code expired with it."

One example that illustrates the meaning of "general equity" concerns the Old Testament law that homeowners put a fence around their roofs. That's because the flat roofs served as sleeping areas and living rooms, especially during hot months, and the goal was to protect life and limb. One equivalent today, when many roofs are pitched and most are not used for parties, is to place fences around swimming pools.

Nuance 7:
Defense and Offense

Free from having to defend a particular piece of land, and free from having to maintain ceremonial laws or the judicial laws of ancient Israel, what should Christians still defend and how should it be defended? That is exactly the question the Jerusalem Council of the early New Testament church had to decide when Paul returned to the central city with news that non-Jews were coming to faith in Christ. Church leader James suggested a three-part answer: "abstain from the things polluted by idols, and from sexual immorality, and from what has been strangled and from blood" (Acts 15:20, English Standard Version).

Other apostles and elders agreed with him, and that became the official church policy. The Jerusalem Council sent a letter to Antioch, where Gentiles were becoming Christians, noting that "it has seemed good to the Holy Spirit and to us to lay on you no greater burden than these requirements. . . . If you keep yourselves from these, you will do well." The Council was trying to keep newcomers from thinking that Christianity (or, at that time, their new perspective on Judaism) was primarily about law rather than grace.

But, as we have seen over the centuries, abstaining from sexual immorality is more easily suggested than done. Look at Paul's insistence to the Corinthian Christians, living in one of the Roman Empire's most dissolute cities, that they purify themselves "from everything that contaminates body and spirit, perfecting holiness out of reverence for God." (II Corinthians 7:1). He similarly told the Ephesians that they "must no longer live as the Gentiles" who "indulge in every kind of impurity, with a continual lust for more" (Ephesians 4:17–19).

Churches, wherever their locations, were and are to be the new holy lands. During Christianity's early history that emphasis seemed to have an impact: In the second century Aristides wrote that Christians "walk in all humility and kindness, and falsehood is not found among them, and they love one another. They despise not the widow and grieve not the orphan." Justin Martyr wrote, "Those who once delighted in fornication now embrace chastity alone." Both Aristides and Justin Martyr were promoting Christianity, but critics also took notice. Tertullian, for example, was impressed by "how they love one another and are ready to die for each other."

As Christianity spread, believers lived in many lands, yet proper conduct among them did not change from one place to another: in every country, husbands and wives were to be faithful to each other out of faithfulness to God, not out of governmental coercion. Christianity has almost always stressed the centrality of the heart, the desire of the individual to follow Christ through God's grace and not external pressure. Once a culture has to resort to blue laws to enforce Sabbath rest, the battle is already largely lost. Obedience has to be volitional or it will not last, and rules enacted to enforce obedience typically provoke resentment.

Today, while many Christians work hard to promulgate laws designed to improve societal morality, many churches are far from being holy lands. Pollster George Barna has compared the total U.S. population with the 35–43 percent of Americans who call themselves "born-again" and the 7–8 percent of the population who are theologically orthodox evangelicals. He found divorce rates about the same, with most of the divorces among born-agains coming after they accepted Christ.

Ron Sider provides a story about one church that is all too common: "a man and a woman from two different married couples had an affair, divorced their spouses, married each other, and assumed they could continue in good standing in the congregation in spite of their defiance of Jesus' teaching and the destruction of two families. Not even in this blatant case of stark disobedience could this evangelical congregation muster the courage to exercise church discipline."

And yet, all is not lost. A journalistic cliché, when trying to learn what's really going on, is "follow the money." One recent survey showed that even though only 9 percent of evangelicals tithe, they do give away twice as much money as the average American, and a third more than mainline church members—4 percent of income rather than 2 percent or 3 percent.

Massive improvements are elusive but small changes are evident. A government-funded study of 12,000 adolescents with some church connection showed that 88 percent of those who had taken a "True Love Waits" pledge not to have sexual relations before marriage had broken the pledge at some point over a six-year period. Nevertheless, girls who took the pledge delayed their age for first having sex from 16.7 years to 19.9 years. Principal investigator Peter Bearman, the chair of Columbia University's sociology department, concluded that "the delay effect is substantial and almost impossible to erase. Taking a pledge delays intercourse for a long time."

Correlations between church involvement and resistance to wrongful activity are particularly strong in inner-city areas, where the difference between the churched and unchurched in everything from arrests to crisis pregnancies has been well-researched both statistically and anecdotally.[2] Given sin within and lures without, churches will never become pure holy lands for the same reason the original Holy Land was unsuccessful. And yet, churches can certainly do more and show more, not by setting up new rules but by affecting hearts through preaching, teaching, worship, and the practice of compassion.

Nuance 8:
Adding, Not Subtracting, in Ten Commandments Cases

As noted earlier, Texas Attorney General Greg Abbott, out of his Christian and constitutional understanding, developed an approach to Ten Commandments monuments far different than that of Judge Moore in Alabama. When Abbott appeared before the U.S. Supreme Court to present his oral defense of the monument near the state capitol building in Austin, he did so in a way deliberately designed not to enrage Supreme Court secularists.

Abbott noted that the Fraternal Order of Eagles donated the monument in 1961 and that lawmakers accepted it "to commend the Eagles for their efforts in fighting juvenile delinquency—a constitutionally secular reason in the court's eyes." He argued that "the Ten Commandments are undoubtedly a sacred religious text, but they are also a foundational document in the development of Western legal codes and culture." He also pointed out that hanging inside the Texas capitol building is the seal of the Republic of Mexico, which "contains an eagle holding a serpent in its mouth, perched on a cactus that grows from a rock surrounded by water. A representation of Aztec mythology, this religious display is neither Jewish nor Christian, but is an acknowledgment of the historical and cultural contributions made by people of differing faiths."

This is important: Here was an attorney general who is a firm Christian saying that Christians can live in a land filled with anti-Christian emblems without being forced theologically to attempt to eliminate them. Here was a Christian saying that a Christian monument could be one among many monuments—and the Supreme Court, after ducking Ten Commandments cases for twenty-five years and refusing to hear Judge Moore's appeal, listened to Abbott (who already had a favorable decision from the Fifth Circuit) and ruled in his favor.

Moore vigorously attacked Abbott as essentially a sub-Christian traitor whose case "den[ied] the sovereignty of God while my case was predicated upon that acknowledgement." Abbott, Moore said, displayed "hypocrisy and lack of faith" by "trying to justify a display of God's law as only secular in nature and in no way representative of the true God." Moore contended that the Supreme Court's 5–4 willingness to let the Texas monument remain was "a devastating loss for America," since to win the case on the grounds of the Commandments' historical significance was to deny their religious significance.

This is a theological debate. If America is the new Israel, Moore is right. If America is a land of religious diversity, Moore is wrong, and Abbott's defense of the Texas monument as a tool for teaching history can be expanded. On the same day that the Supreme Court allowed the Texas monument it upheld the Sixth Circuit Court's order that framed copies of the Commandments be removed from the walls of two Kentucky county courthouses and a public school, since the decalogues were placed there with obvious religious intent. And yet, that same court ruling suggests an opportunity to add rather than to subtract.

In his ruling Judge Eric Clay wrote that merely posting the Ten Commandments fulfilled no "educational function," but he also opined that the outcome of the case may have been different had the Ten Commandments been "integrated into the school curriculum." The judge alluded to previous U.S. Supreme Court musings that the Ten Commandments have a place "in an appropriate study of history, civilization, ethics. . . ." He suggested that the court could look favorably on a display if the Ten Commandments were incorporated into a comparative religion course or a course on how the founders' religious beliefs affected late-eighteenth-century history and the structure of the U.S. government.

The U.S. Supreme Court did not take a position on such speculation, but

Christians should. Wouldn't it make sense for Ten Commandments proponents to work harder on day-in, day-out teaching rather than on merely putting up a display? Why not stipulate that, as part of their "core knowledge," all children should know the Ten Commandments as well as the central points of the Magna Carta and the Declaration of Independence, just as they should know where the fifty states are located? Why not place in school lobbies memory aids, such as Ten Commandments displays and maps of the United States, that support classroom teaching?

Courts might balk at that, but the debate then would be about teaching minds rather than about symbolically claiming a piece of ground or a building. Christians would be on the side of adding substance to the curriculum, and letting principals and teachers figure out how to fit it in, rather than lobbying to subtract ("censor") what they do not like. Similarly, when the University of North Carolina assigned portions of the Koran as part of freshman orientation, Christians should not have objected; instead, they should have pushed for inclusion of parts of the Bible as well.

Nuance 9:
The Debate Concerning Same-Sex Marriage

Addition, not subtraction, has its limits: Christians cannot happily add same-sex marriage to our culture for the same reason we cannot smile on abortion, but on this issue as well we need to explain that same-sex marriage is really not an extension of liberty, although it may seem that way in the short run. Seana Segrue, in a paper presented at a December 2003 conference hosted by the Witherspoon Fellowship, pointed out that the same-sex marriage movement is a subset of a sexual revolution based in liberty, but liberty "achieved through the empowerment of a state with the strength to destroy sexual norms, and hence the institution of marriage as the foundation of the family wherein children are primarily socialized and learn to be self-governing."

She noted that "lacking roots in biology, in tradition, in a sense of duty, same-sex marriage is not sufficiently resilient to fend off the vicissitudes which the ordinary and extraordinary demands of life place upon all of us. Being entirely a creation of the state, it is an institution that needs to be coddled, and which demands cocooning to protect it. . . . It is desperately in need of state intervention to support it. . . . The need of same-sex unions to be culturally coddled also increases the likelihood that the state will use public education for this end." We are already seeing that to be the case: students need to be reeducated to see as regular what almost all instinctively recognize as irregular.

Same-sex marriage can be made to seem normal only if we subtract both educational freedom and religious liberty. Professor Segrue again: "The state necessarily stands in opposition to religious institutions that refuse to recognize same-sex marriage, and this opposition is heightened by the fact that same-sex marriage is in need of a protective culture to be sustainable." The new imperative "indicts religious institutions that stand in opposition to same-sex marriage as intolerant. Through this charge, the moral authority of religious institutions is undermined in the eyes of the public who are encouraged to view uncompromising faiths as unreasonable and unsupportive of marriage," as it has been redefined.

This redlining of religious institutions has a further effect: "Parents, raising children in a society in which religion is widely regarded as inconsistent with official public policy, are less apt to expose their children to it. Parents thereby choose to deprive themselves of a fundamental support for their own marriages." If the state then declares opposition to homosexuality a form of "hate speech," churches will have to decide whether to remain true to the tenets of their faith or, as in the official church system of China, sue for peace with a government that is happy to indulge churches as long as they undergo an extreme makeover.

We could speculate as well about other consequences, but here's the essence: "The right to do whatever one wants to do can only exist in a society that removes all impediments and tidies up the social dislocations and inconveniences created by the sexual indulgence of its members." What looks like addition in the short run ends up as subtraction, because same-sex marriage goes so much against human nature that a backlash will inevitably occur—and then the state will have to squash that backlash to preserve the status of a favored group.

I want to stress that same-sex marriage must be opposed, but in a way that treats homosexuals as still possessing human dignity. Biblically, any posture that implies, "I'm righteous and you're not," or suggests that homosexuality is the worst of all problems, displays an inadequate view of sin. In January 2006, a positive movie about missionaries, *End of the Spear*, hit movie theaters, but a few Christians demanded that the movie be boycotted because it turned out that an actor who played one of the missionaries is a homosexual. That campaign was sad in its assault on a powerful movie with strong biblical content, but also inconsistent unless the boycotters also attacked movies with actors who are heterosexual adulterers.

Marvin Olasky

Nuance 10:
We, the Neighbors

Expansive, nondefensive Christianity has been the outstanding vehicle in human history for increasing the liberty of those seen as subhuman until Christians began viewing them as neighbors: women, the poor, the sick, racial and ethnic minorities, and now the not-yet-born. Certainly, some Christians defended slavery and discrimination, but they were doing what was common in much of the world: The sensational news was that a critical mass of Christians fought for what was uncommon and opposed state-sponsored slavery and racial discrimination. The evangelistic desire to add rather than subtract was essential, for a willingness to take risks led to "We, the people" including more and more people.

The big nineteenth-century experiment was whether the "we" could include different religions. President George Washington had signaled a coming expansion in 1789 when he wrote to one synagogue, "May the children of the stock of Abraham who dwell in this land continue to merit and enjoy the good will of the other inhabitants, while everyone shall sit in safety under his own vine and fig tree and there shall be none to make him afraid." In 1800, though, the U.S. was still an almost entirely Protestant country. Then, millions of Catholic immigrants arrived from Ireland, Italy, Poland, and other countries. Later in the century, millions of Jews arrived from Eastern Europe.

Ugly nativist groups sprung up, of course, and some Christians sadly joined them, for some Protestants who thought of their country as a holy land fought what they saw as pollution by millions of immigrants with non-Protestant faiths. Nevertheless, by the end of the century the consensus was clear: *We the neighbors* include Catholics and Jews, and soon there was a smattering of Buddhists, Hindus, and Muslims as well.

The big twentieth-century experiment was whether the "we" could include different racial and ethnic groups. The Civil War hadn't settled that, since African Americans largely moved from slavery to sharecropping, which did not leave many materially better off. In the mid-twentieth century, though, strong and courageous Christians (once again, sadly, with exceptions) fought for civil rights as many of their predecessors had fought for emancipation. In India, Hindu priests led the opposition to equal rights for the dark-skinned Dalits ("untouchables"), but in the United States ministers like Martin Luther King and others of the Southern Christian Leadership Conference demanded that African Americans be treated as neighbors.

That drive for addition was successful, but others have not been. Many by inaction or misguided action subtracted the poor from the list of neighbors, but compassionate conservatives in recent years have insisted on treating the poor as part of the "we" who are capable of working, marrying, and building families. Compassionate conservatism is the modern manifestation of biblical compassion. Christians have also insisted that unborn children are part of the "we," despite the Supreme Court's attempt in *Roe v. Wade* to exclude them.

Christians defend human life on biblical grounds, but also on the grounds, completely open to nonbelievers, that the unborn and the newborn are part of "We, the people." One woman who had an abortion wrote of how "there just wasn't room" in her life for the child growing within her, so she aborted her child and realized later that she could have made room. She wrote, "I have this ghost now. A very little ghost that only appears when I'm seeing something beautiful, like the full moon on the ocean last weekend. And the baby waves at me. And I wave at the baby."[3]

Addition can lift us onto high moral ground. Subtraction yields ghosts. Christians can be strong and courageous by bringing faith to the marketplace and governmental halls and into homes and offices, by looking for opportunities to debate rather than debase opponents, and by emphasizing the opportunities to add rather than subtract.

As churches become models they can move onto offense with great flexibility, keeping in mind a frequent biblical metaphor: Christians as salt. It's an apt usage not only because salt is both a preservative and a flavoring, but because the two elements that make up salt—NaCl, sodium and chlorine—are both poisonous when ingested by themselves. The key teaching of Christianity is that God saves sinners. A holy God saves sinful man through his merciful action, so Christians should try to communicate both God's holiness and his mercy, remembering that holiness without love is acidic, and love without holiness is cloyingly over-sweet.

Salty activists do not overdose on just one of the elements. For example, a Christian demonstration outside an abortion business should declare both that abortion is wrong and that God is merciful to aborters and abortionists who come to faith in him. Protesters who seem hateful to troubled women because they appear to offer condemnation rather than hope are not helping the cause of Christ. The type of strength and courage most needed today is evident at the front lines of poverty-fighting and pro-life work throughout the world. Two of my heroes are Jim and Terry Cooney of Maryland, who have adopted numerous children with a variety of physical and mental difficulties, and have loved them all.

The ABCs of Conservative Christian Leadership

Because Joshua in the Bible showed one type of strength and courage as he led his troops into hostile territory, some Christians today think in military terms as well, but they need to ask themselves whether they are following Christ or enjoying the adrenaline rush that rage produces. Rage, like alcohol, can make us feel stronger, more courageous, and more powerful, but James and other New Testament writers noted that the wrath of man does not accomplish the righteousness of God. Paul had it right in his much-quoted verse: "If I speak in the tongues of men and of angels, but have not love, I am a noisy gong or a clanging cymbal" (I Corinthians 13).

Corinthian Christians, living in an ungodly port city, could have unendingly protested the decadence around them, but Paul pleaded with them to show love, which he defined as "not arrogant or rude. It does not insist on its own way; it is not irritable or resentful. . . . When I was a child, I spoke like a child, I thought like a child, I reasoned like a child. When I became a man, I gave up childish ways."

Christians need to give up both childish tactics of the kind Paul redlines and childish strategies that sometimes bring pet issues to the forefront. Some issues—religious liberty, marriage, life—are essential ones, but others are discretionary and require prudential judgment. For ease of memory we can even set up an ABC of how to decide which discretionary issues to emphasize:

Assess accurately both past and present. Western civilization is founded on both Jerusalem and Athens, biblical and classical knowledge, and just as it is not accurate for liberal professors to ignore the Bible, so it is not accurate for conservative Christians to say that nonbiblical strains were unimportant in the formation of Western civilization or America itself. Christianity was crucial in the founding of the United States, but some deists and skeptics also were part of the revolutionary coalition—and that means we should not look upon America as a holy land lost and strive to return to the early days. Each era has sin sufficient unto itself.

Build consensus among conservative Christians. The Calvinist concept that "lesser magistrates" can sometimes rebel against a tyrannical government—in the American context, local and state officials standing up against federal over-reaching—is a mighty one, but "magistrates" is plural, not singular. Individual rebellion can be quirky, so the requirement that many magistrates agree on the need for change makes sure that the grievances are great. Our key opponents are secular liberals, not other conservatives, and rhetoric that divides us helps our adversaries to conquer.

Choose battles and tactics carefully. Sometimes we have no choice of battleground; if we are ordered to stop praying to God or to bow to idols, we must stand firm wherever we are, as did Daniel and his friends in ancient Babylon. When we do have a choice, though, we should seize opportunities to build winning alliances, and not rush toward martyrdom when other God-honoring options exist. (Otherwise, it's not martyrdom, but suicide.)

If we follow these ABCs, we will not adopt the terrible tactic of spam recruitment: making statements that excite one listener but turn off a thousand. Those who with a defeatist mentality assume that minds cannot change, so the only goal is to propel into action those already in your camp, are like spam e-mailers: They don't care how many get irritated as long as a sale is made. That hurts not only Christian social and political activity but evangelism as well, and underestimates God's ability to change hearts.

In the end, Christians should not tear apart the Reagan coalition of libertarians and conservative Christians nor abandon the goal of advancing both liberty and virtue. We should not send eviction notices to those who do not agree with all of our ideas. God wanted Gideon's army to be small, but that was based on special revelation. Today, efforts designed to create a tiny hard core by rejecting others owe more to Lenin than to the Bible. Benjamin Franklin's quip, despite its frequent quotation, should always remain fresh in our minds: We must hang together so that we do not hang separately.

8

From Reagan Democrats to Social Conservatives: Hard Choices Facing the Pro-Family Cause

Allan C. Carlson

IN THIS BOOK, WE honor the legacy of Ronald Reagan by considering the future of American conservatism. My contribution will focus on the pro-family movement in an attempt to help answer two important questions: Why, for the first three decades of his adult life, was Ronald Reagan a Democrat? And why, during the 1960s, did he become a Republican? I will also examine the current state, and possible future, of the social-conservative, or pro-family, cause within the Republican ranks.

Why Was Ronald Reagan Once a Democrat?

Let us go back about one hundred years. The first openly pro-family American president was a Republican, Theodore Roosevelt. A man of keen intelligence, he was also a close student of U.S. Census numbers. As he pored over reports from 1890, 1900, and 1910, Roosevelt identified troubling signs. The U.S. marriage rate was falling. As the Reno divorce mills opened up in Nevada, the divorce rate shot up. Meanwhile, the marital birthrate fell by 25 percent over these years, marking a sharp American retreat from the business of having children. Roosevelt commented on the huge disruption in home life caused by the rise of a factory civilization, which separated the workplace from the home and also separated working mothers and fathers from each other and from their children for the largest share of the day. The great new challenge, he believed, was to save the home as a center of autonomy and freedom.

In response, Roosevelt called for an open pro-family politics. "[I]t is in the life of the family," he wrote, "upon which in the last analysis the whole welfare of the nation rests." Addressing women, he said that no nation "can exist at all" unless the average woman was "the home-keeper, the good wife, and unless she is the mother of a sufficient number of healthy children" to keep the nation "going forward." Addressing fathers, he declared that their "primary task" was to earn their own livelihoods and "the livelihoods of those dependent" on them. Accordingly, he embraced the principle of the family wage, which held that the emerging industrial sector could claim one, but only one, family member, the father, who deserved a family-sustaining wage in return. Mothers and children would be free at home. This system also built on cultural assumptions regarding "men's jobs" (marked by higher wages and salaries and long-term tenure) and "women's jobs" (oriented to lower pay and short-term tenure).

All the same, Roosevelt stressed that true marriage was "a partnership of the soul, the spirit and the mind, no less than of the body" and that the "highest ideal of the family" could be obtained "only where the father and the mother stand to each other as lovers and friends." The Roughrider also blasted what he called the "foes of our household," including the birth-control movement, equity feminism, eugenics, and liberal Christianity. Addressing a group of progressive Christian theologians, for example, he equated Americanism with the willingness to bear children:

> If you do not believe in your own [people] enough, to wish to see [their numbers] kept up, then you are not good Americans, you are not patriots; and . . . I for one shall not mourn your extinction; and in such event I shall welcome the advent of a new race that will take your place, because you will have shown that you are not fit to cumber the ground.

It is hard to imagine a contemporary political leader being so honest, or so bold. Even so, Theodore Roosevelt was the only prominent Republican of his era to think and talk in this way. The dominant wing of the GOP tilted in favor of the banks and the great industries, protecting the interests of high finance and the National Association of Manufacturers. As early as 1904, the manufacturers group had formed a tacit alliance with the feminist movement to subvert the family-wage ideal. The feminists wanted women— all women—out of the home, in full-time employment, as the only road to what they saw as true equality. Seeking to lower labor costs, the manufacturers also wanted free access to the labor of all women, single or married, arguing that "no limitation should be placed upon the opportunities of any person to learn any trade to which he or she may be adapted." When the equity feminist movement reorganized as the National Women's Party in 1917, it appears that the manufacturers actually lent their secret financial support.

Meanwhile, the Republican Party gave political encouragement to the feminists, as well. When the National Women's Party crafted its proposed Equal Rights Amendment in 1923, the manufacturers association was the first group to endorse it and Republican leaders were the chief sponsors in both the House and the Senate. Moreover, the Republican Party was the first to endorse the ERA in its national platform. This linkage of feminism to big business and to the Republican Party was actually a natural and strong alliance. A little later, after the Birth Control League of America cleverly changed its name to Planned Parenthood, it too found a cozy home in the Republican Party. By the 1950s, Planned Parenthood was a favored charity among Republican Women's Clubs.

Meanwhile, the Democrats consolidated their nineteenth-century legacy of "Rum, Romanism, and Rebellion": that is, their position as the party favorable to cultural pluralism, new immigrants, southern agrarians, northern Catholics, small property, and family wages for male workers. Joining them in the early twentieth century were a group of women sometimes called the social feminists, but better labeled Maternalists. They included Julia Lathrop, Florence Kelley, Frances Perkins, Grace Abott, Mary Anderson, Frances Kellor, Katherine Lenroot, and Molly Dewson. While believing strongly in equal legal and political rights for women and men, the Maternalists emphasized the natural differences between the sexes when it came to childbearing and nurturing. They held that the first duty of all women was to protect infant life and to nurture children, that employment outside the home was inconsistent with good mothering, that public policy should provide special protections for mothers and children, and that the "family wage" for fathers was the central pillar of social welfare and economic justice.

The Maternalists—backed heavily by Democratic votes—were responsible for creating in 1912, as part of the Department of Commerce and Labor, the U.S. Children's Bureau. The new Bureau focused on "baby-saving": what a wonderful goal for a federal program! It published trailblazing booklets on prenatal care and infant care; created Little Mothers Leagues in urban centers where girls learned about baby feeding and rearing; promoted breastfeeding; and convened National Baby Week in 1916, which involved 4,200 communities, complete with "best baby" contests and parades featuring mothers with infants-in-arms. The Bureau celebrated "The Year of the Child" in 1918, a campaign to promote good mothering and reduce infant mortality that mobilized an amazing eleven million women, a third of the nation's adult female population.

Other Maternalist policy victories included the Smith-Lever Extension Act of 1914, which launched the 4-H and Homemakers movements, and the Smith-Hughes Vocational Training Act of 1917, which provided federal funds to school districts for the training of girls in home economics. While there were technical sides to these initiatives, their spirit is best captured by the song "Dreaming," included in *The 4-H Songbook* of 1928 (here, the third verse):

> My home must have its mother,
> May I grow sweet and wise;
> My home must have its father,
> With honor in his eyes;
> My home must have its children,
> God grant the parents grace
> To keep our home through all the years
> A kindly, happy place.

I emphasize that this generically Christian, pleasantly pro-family vision represented federally engineered education under the domain of the Maternalists. In 1945, the U.S. Department of Agriculture expanded the initiative, creating Future Homemakers of America. Within a decade, this high school club had over 600,000 active members.

Still another Maternalist victory was passage of the Sheppard-Towner Act in 1921. As the first true "entitlement" ever approved by Congress, Sheppard-Towner also aimed at "baby-saving," this time through programs such as visiting nurses and prenatal care designed to reduce maternal and infant mortality. Predictably, the American Medical Association fiercely opposed Sheppard-Towner, calling it "sob stuff."

More surprisingly, the Democrats' New Deal of the 1930s also represented a triumph for the Maternalists. A contemporary sign of this is the uniform loathing of the New Deal shown by all recent feminist historians. For example, Mimi Abramovitz condemns the New Deal because it "upheld patriarchal social arrangements," while Alice Kessler-Harris attacks Franklin Roosevelt's program for "locking men and women into rigid attitudes" and for "stifling a generation of feminist thought."

Why this reaction? The answer is simple. Every New Deal domestic program either openly built on or assumed a "family wage" model. The domestic ideal behind the New Deal was a nation composed of family homes with breadwinning fathers, stay-at-home mothers, and little flocks of children. Every economic, welfare, and social insurance measure adopted during the

1930s aimed at reinforcing this modest patriarchal order. The goal was openly pursued. As one of the technical architects of the Social Security Act, Abraham Epstein, wrote in 1933:

> It must be remembered that the American standard assumes a normal family of man, wife, and two or three children, with the father fully able to provide for them out of his own income. This standard presumes no supplementary earnings from either the wife or young children.

How did it work in practice? Take the largest unemployment relief program, the Works Progress Administration. Participation was limited to one breadwinner per family; 85 percent of the 4.5 million enrollees were men. Those women who were in the program found themselves assigned to "sewing rooms" and to classes on child care, cooking, and home health. Or consider the Social Security Amendments of 1939, the true crown jewel of the New Deal, which gave to working men (but *not* to working women) new, family-oriented benefits: an extra pension for homemaking wives and fairly generous survivors benefits to widows (but not to widowers) and their children.

Ronald Reagan proudly voted four times for Franklin D. Roosevelt. All his life, he expressed admiration for the domestic programs of the New Deal, a fact which has puzzled some conservatives. From the "family" perspective, though, this makes perfect sense. The Democratic Party of FDR and the New Deal was the party of the traditional family; the Republicans, relatively speaking, were the party of feminism and corporate interests. I believe that the New Deal project premised on a "family wage" system, when combined with tax reforms in 1944 and 1948 and generous home mortgage subsidies for young families, created the material conditions that made possible the "marriage" and "baby" booms of the 1940s and 1950s. While Dwight Eisenhower reaped the credit, this family-centered era was primarily the policy achievement of the Democrats.

Why Did Ronald Reagan Become a Republican?

Strange ideas began to swirl within the Democratic Party early in the 1960s. Relative to the family, the key date was February 8, 1964, when the Maternalist movement mounted its last stand and a radical form of equity feminism broke into the party's ranks.

Under debate that day was Title VII of the Civil Rights Act of 1964, which dealt with employment issues. As originally drafted by the Lyndon Johnson White House, the underlying purpose of Title VII was to open up job opportunities for black males so that they could earn a "family wage" and become stable husbands and fathers. As Edith Green, a Democrat from Oregon, would explain: "Whether we want to admit it or not, the main purpose of this legislation today is to try to end the discrimination . . . against [male] Negroes." Accordingly, this initiative fit well into the Maternalist worldview and mission.

However, the so-called Dixiecrats—Southern Democrats opposed to the entire Civil Rights Act—turned, with their backs to the wall, to a dangerous strategy. Howard Smith, a Democrat from Virginia, rose on the floor of the House and proposed adding "sex" to the list of prohibited discriminations under Title VII. It appears that he and his Southern colleagues saw this as a killer amendment, one that would reveal the dangers lurking within the "equality" principle. Or perhaps they saw it as a way to push aside the intended beneficiaries of Title VII—black males—by turning legal attention to the job claims of vastly more numerous white females.

In any case, the equity feminists in the Republican Party—including Representatives Katherine St. George of New York and Catharine May of Washington—rallied behind their at times whimsical, at times bewildered, Dixiecrat colleagues. In opposition, "New Deal" Democrats, committed to the defense of the traditional family, raised their collective voice for the last time. For example, Emmanuel Cellar—liberal Democrat, Manhattanite, Jewish, and chairman of the House Judiciary Committee—defended in this debate the natural inequality of women and men:

> You know, the French have a phrase for it when they speak of
> women and men . . . "vive la difference." I think the French are
> right. Imagine the upheaval that would result from the adoption
> of blanket language requiring total [sexual] equality. Would male
> citizens be justified in insisting that women share with them the
> burdens of compulsory military service? What would become of
> traditional family relationships? What about alimony?

These were important questions which would haunt the future. Other Maternalist Democrats insisted that the real "biological differences" between men and women needed to be recognized in employment law, in order to protect mothers and the best interests of children.

The "new" voice in the Democratic Party came from Representative Martha Griffiths of Michigan. She referred to an ideologically charged appendix to Gunnar Myrdal's well-known 1944 book, *American Dilemma: The Negro Problem and American Democracy*. The volume itself had focused on American race relations, especially the practice of segregation in the South.

Allan C. Carlson

The appendix to which Rep. Griffith referred, though, had been authored by Mrydal's wife, Alva. It argued, in Griffith's words, "that white women and Negroes occupy relatively the same position in American society." Both, she said, were suppressed by white males. If unamended, Griffiths insisted, Title VII would leave "white men in one bracket" and give equal employment rights to "colored men and colored women," while "down at the bottom of the list is going to be a white woman with no rights at all."

In response, Maternalist Democrats warned that the whole panoply of labor laws protecting women and mothers and those Social Security provisions premised on the male breadwinner/female homemaker model would be destroyed by this amendment. However, the strange coalition formed that day of Southern Dixiecrats, feminist Republicans, and the new arch-feminist Democrats prevailed, by a vote of 168 to 133. While the process of deconstruction took another decade or so to complete, America's "family wage" regime entered its death throes.

Great political transformations are rarely simple and clean. A decade would pass before the Democratic Party became clearly identified as the party of the sexual revolution in America, celebrating birth control, abortion, "new family forms," and homosexuality. The transformation of the Republican Party into the party of the family took even longer. Ronald Reagan, our subject here, formally became a Republican in 1962, driven largely it seems by national security concerns. As governor of California, Reagan still signed measures into law during the late 1960s that liberalized access to abortion and implemented "no fault" divorce. Later, he regretted these acts, but they were very much in line with the worldview of the old Republican Party. Indeed, it is fair to say that following the collapse of the Maternalist Democrats in 1964, the traditional family had no meaningful political defenders at all for nearly a decade.

A "pro-family" Republican Party only developed during the mid-1970s, a change that went hand-in-hand with the emergence of the modern "pro-family" movement and the so-called Reagan Democrats. The Supreme Court's January 1973 decision in *Roe v. Wade*, overturning the abortion laws of all fifty states, disturbed many. However, the first crystallizing event was the Mondale-Brademus bill of 1973, which would have created a massive day-care entitlement embracing all American preschool children. Conservative Catholic pioneers such as Paul Weyrich and Connie Marshner organized grassroots opposition to this massive federal power grab over the young. Meanwhile, in desperation, some Republicans found their pro-family voices. Senator Carl Curtis of Nebraska accused social planners of tearing children from their families and mothers, while Representative John Schmitz of California declared that "A Nation of orphanages cannot endure, and should not. It is an offense to God and men." The old Maternalist wing of the Democratic Party had strongly opposed day care of any sort; the Democratic Party of the 1970s gave this turn to social parenting overwhelming support, and Congress approved the bill. The hero here turned out to be Richard Nixon, who successfully vetoed the measure. It appears that a young presidential aide, Patrick Buchanan, drafted the veto message, which stated: "For the federal government to plunge headlong . . . into supporting child development would commit the vast moral authority of the federal government to the side of communal approaches to child rearing as against the family-centered approach."

The other notable pro-family pioneer was Phyllis Schlafly, who, in a stunning upset, led the campaign that defeated the Equal Rights Amendment. A Catholic wife, mother, and lawyer, Schlafly had first come to public attention with her 1964 book, *A Choice, Not an Echo*, a tribute to Barry Goldwater. Just as with Ronald Reagan, her principle concern at the time was national defense. However, in 1971, the ERA—first proposed by the National Woman's Party and its Republican friends back in 1923—finally won approval in Congress and went out to the states, where all observers expected quick ratification. Schlafly first editorialized against the ERA in February 1972, arguing that it would force women into the military draft, to serve in combat, and to lose financial protection as wives and mothers. That September, she gathered one hundred friends—mostly from Republican women's clubs—to meet in St. Louis, where they launched the Stop-ERA campaign. In 1976, with ERA advocates only two states short of ratification, she reached out to the churches, drawing a thousand mainline Protestants, evangelicals, Catholics, Mormons, and Orthodox Jews to an anti-ERA rally in Springfield, Illinois. "That is when the pro-family movement was invented," she reports.

Politically, the group that would soon be called "the Reagan Democrats" first became visible in the 1972 presidential election. Richard Nixon publicly declared his opposition to easy abortion and won 59 percent of the Catholic vote— a record for a Republican—and also made deep inroads into the evangelical South. The 1976 campaign occurred under the shadow of the Watergate scandal, and Democratic candidate Jimmy Carter cleverly reverted to old Maternalist language, pledging to establish a national commission to "save the American family." Many Catholics and evangelicals returned to the Democratic fold. However, reflecting new Democratic Party realities, Carter's eventual White House Conference on families—note the change to the plural "Families" here— degenerated into a broad attack on the natural family and the celebration of new family forms, including single-parent and homosexual varieties.

This set the stage for the election of 1980. Ronald Reagan reclaimed the Catholic vote and also won dramatic gains in the South. The greatest swing occurred among ethnic Catholics—Irish, Italians, Poles, and Slovaks—who gave him overwhelming support. For example, he won 64 percent of Italian-

Catholics in California. The "Reagan Democrats" were now solidly in the Republican camp. The GOP had reclaimed the pro-family legacy of Teddy Roosevelt. Reagan himself explained his victory to a group of Catholic voters in this way:

> The secret is that when the Left took over the Democratic Party we [former Democrats] took over the Republican Party. We made the Republican Party into the Party of the working people, the family, the neighborhood, the defense of freedom, and yes, the American Flag and the Pledge of Allegiance to one Nation Under God. So, you see, the Party that so many of us grew up with still exists except that today it's called the Republican Party.

The Republican Party and the Traditional Family: An Appraisal

Allow me to turn to another question: How well has the Republican Party actually performed as the party of the traditional family?

At the level of party platform, fairly well. Since 1980, pro-family and pro-life activists have successfully produced Republican platforms that have opposed ratification of the Equal Rights Amendment; endorsed a constitutional amendment to overturn *Roe v. Wade* and protect preborn infant life; called for pro-family tax policies; and so on. And there have been concrete wins.

In tax policy, for example the Tax Reform Act of 1986 doubled the value of the child-friendly personal exemption and indexed it to inflation. A 1996 reform created a new Child Tax Credit, initially set at $400. George Bush's 2001 tax cut raised this credit to $1,000 and began to eliminate the tax code's notorious marriage penalty.

There have been other gains. Congress has approved and President Bush has signed a ban on partial-birth abortion. The welfare reform of 1996 eliminated perverse incentives for out-of-wedlock births. Under George W. Bush, both domestic and foreign "population policies" have shifted in pro-life, pro-family directions. At present, the Administration for Children, Youth, and Families and the Office for Population Affairs, important branches of the Department of Health and Human Services, are in pro-family hands. As of February 2006, so is the State Department's Bureau of Population, Refugees, and Migration. Judges with pro-family and pro-life records have won presidential appointment to federal courts (most recently Samuel Alito and John Roberts). Especially with the current Republican administration, "social conservatives" have felt that they hold a true seat at the table.

Even so, all is not well with the existing Republican coalition. Indeed, there are other indicators that the Republican Party has done relatively little to help traditional families. Certainly at the level of net incomes, the one-earner family today is worse off than it was thirty years ago when the Republican Party began to claim the pro-family banner. Specifically, the median income of married-couple families, with the wife not in the paid labor force, was only $40,100 in 2002, less than it was in 1970 ($40,785) when inflation is taken into account. In contrast, the real earnings of two-income married-couple families rose by 35 percent over the same period, to nearly $73,000. As the Maternalists had long warned, eliminating America's family wage system has driven male wages down and severely handicapped the one-income home.

Despite economic pressures, though, such families are not extinct. They still constitute core "social conservative" constituencies—for example, homeschooling families and large families with four or more children. But they have little to show from the years of Republican domination. Indeed, Republicans have done virtually nothing to control the egalitarian frenzy and gender-role engineering set off by Title VII of the Civil Rights Act and Title IX of the Education Amendments of 1972.

Consider child care. Richard Nixon's veto stopped the day-care juggernaut in 1973, but only for a few months. The same year, Congress approved and Nixon signed another measure backed by the National Organization for Women—the heir to the National Woman's Party. This law allowed families to deduct day-care costs from their income taxes, cleverly labeling them as "business expenses." Within a few years Congress passed a new measure, with bipartisan support, creating a 20 percent tax credit for day-care expenses. This has since grown into a credit worth between $1,500 and $2,100 in reduced taxes for families buying child care. Even the wealthiest households qualify. Meanwhile, families that sacrifice a second income to keep a mother—or father—at home full-time receive no recognition and pay *higher* net taxes. Bills to correct this gross inequity have been regularly introduced since 1996, but have gone nowhere in the Republican-controlled Congress.

Or look at the recent bankruptcy reform measure, approved in 2005. In a nutshell, it makes a "clean start" after filing for bankruptcy much more difficult for a family. Instead, most affected families will find themselves essentially indentured to a bank or credit card bureau, paying off their debt for years or, more probably, decades to come, with little hope of ever starting over. Without question, some had abused the old law, turning repeated bankruptcy filings into a kind of circus. A tightening on this side probably made sense. Significantly, though, the recent reform made no real changes on the lenders' side, measures which might have reined in an increasingly predatory credit industry. It is common knowledge, for example, that credit card companies intentionally urge financially troubled families to borrow still more money, because they can charge extremely high interest rates. "They are the ones who provide most of our profit," one Citibank executive candidly observes.

What do these issues have in common? All three are areas where the interests of big business and the interests of average families collided, and in each case the Republican Party sided in the end with business. Concerning one-income families, the great corporations continue to view them as a waste of human resources, artificially boosting labor costs by holding one adult at home. The GOP quietly ignores their situation. For the same reason, large businesses generally favor federally subsidized day care, for it creates incentives for mothers to work rather than care for their young children, which in turn pushes overall labor costs down. Republican policy strongly favors this social parenting. And the credit industry has every interest in creating a new, indentured debtor class annually sending 20 percent of their income to the banks.

Other family economic issues are looming, with little indication of a Republican willingness to tackle them in a pro-family way. Consider the Federal Student Loan program, launched in the mid-1970s as a modest supplement to means-tested federal education grants. The system has since morphed into a massive debt machine, loaning out $58 billion in 2005 alone and now used by about 70 percent of college and university students. The average bachelor's degree recipient currently graduates with $20,000 in debt; students having attended graduate school report another $50,000 to $100,000 in debt; creating in one commentator's words "the most indebted generation of young Americans ever." Here we find another newly indentured class of Americans, also paying about 20 percent of their incomes to banks or corporations for decades to come. More disturbingly, over 20 percent of these borrowers report that they have delayed having children because of their debt, while 15 percent say they have delayed marriage. These are not pro-family outcomes. The most recent Republican response to the borrower's plight—done in the name of fiscal responsibility—was to pass a measure that would raise interest rates and the long-term debt facing these young adults.

Another looming new issue is Title IV-D of the Social Security Act, the federal government's child support collection and enforcement program. Originally designed to track down the welfare fathers of illegitimate children, the program has increasingly targeted middle-income households affected by divorce. There is mounting evidence that the system now encourages divorce and exacerbates fatherlessness by creating a winner-take-all game wherein the losing parent—commonly a father wanting to save the marriage—is unfairly penalized by the loss of his children and by a federally enforced child support obligation. Here we see still another newly indentured class of citizens under the thumb of the federal government. If you think I exaggerate, I refer you to no less a personage than Phyllis Schlafly, who calls this runaway federal law the most serious danger facing American families today.

Democrats often dream of wooing the "Reagan Democrats" back into the fold. Bill Clinton, who could speak in the idiom of evangelicals and who embraced pro-family tax and welfare reforms, succeeded to some degree. Democratic strategist Stanley Greenberg, who actually coined the phrase "Reagan Democrats," argues that "a new, family-centered politics can define and revitalize the Democratic Party." Its message should highlight "family integrity and parental responsibility" and offer a "progressive vision of family support." Greenberg even theorizes that "Roman Catholics would [again] rally to a Democratic Party respectful of family and committed to defending government's unique role in supporting it."

If the Democratic Party remains the party of the sexual revolution, evidenced most recently in the campaign for gay marriage, such dreams will remain just that. However, if a Democratic leader can ever shake that monkey off his or her back, the prospects for another broad political realignment are strong. For when push comes to shove, social conservatives remain second-class citizens under the Republican tent. During the 2004 Republican convention, social conservatives were almost literally confined to the party's attic, kept off the main stage and treated like slightly lunatic children. Republican lobbyist Michael Scanlon's candid comment—"The wackos get their information [from] the Christian Right [and] Christian radio"—suggests a common opinion among the "K Street" Republicans toward their coalition allies. Contemporary Republican leaders need to do better—much better—toward social conservatives, and they must creatively address pressing new family economic issues, lest they squander the revolutionary political legacy of Ronald Reagan.

9

Stuck-with-Virtue Conservatism

Peter Augustine Lawler

WE HUMAN BEINGS ARE stuck with virtue. And we conservatives defend both the inevitability and goodness of virtue against those who believe that it might be good or might be inevitable that our need for it wither away. We are conservatives because conservatives conserve and liberals liberate. But things do get a little complicated. We American conservatives want to conserve at least some of our liberal tradition, including the revolutionary Declaration of Independence. Human virtue, we believe, is impossible without human liberty.

The model American, from one view, works to conserve a nation dedicated to liberal principles—to the natural rights of free individuals—against their illiberal enemies: monarchists, communists, socialists, progressives, fascists, and fundamentalists, Islamic or even Christian. The only problem with this view—but it is a big one—is that the individual with rights is sometimes portrayed without indispensable and ennobling duties or virtues. So we sometimes quite wrongly think of the goal of liberty as the maximization of individual or unconstrained choice, as if free human beings could become more dignified and happy if only they had the unlimited power to choose for or against virtue, or if every human choice became a matter of calculation, contract, and consent. The truth is that human liberty would be impossible without human virtue, and in the end, liberty serves virtue, and not the other way around.

Conservative liberals—a group that includes many of the neoconservatives—say that liberal politics depends upon conservative sociology, and so what separates a conservative liberal from a liberal liberal is a sensible concern for the perpetuation of the moral supports for liberty. Liberal conservatives, for their part, say that finally our free liberal political institutions make sense only by pointing beyond themselves in the direction of morality, virtue, political responsibility, philosophy, theology, and God, just as the individual's pursuit of happiness makes sense only if it culminates in humanly worthy happiness itself. By understanding ourselves as free individuals we pursue the means of human happiness, but it is as parents, children, friends, lovers, citizens, and creatures that we actually are humanly happy. Liberal conservatives believe that it is not only sensible to accept but wonderful to acknowledge in gratitude that we're stuck with virtue.

Our Enemies: Fascists?

We conservatives must fine-tune the conservative liberals' enemies' list according to our true situation today. (The monarchists have been on the run for a long, long time, and I don't see any reason to disturb their harmless fantasies.) There is a tendency among some fairly conservative liberals—such as Christopher Hitchens—to equate the fascists with today's fundamentalists. But whatever might be true in the Middle East—where the term Islamofascism makes some sense—that connection makes virtually no sense here in our country. The European fascists have been the most rootless and alienated people around, members of a lonely crowd looking for some leader to make sense of their pathetic lives. Fascists begin as individuals in the Tocquevillian or isolated and apathetic sense, disconnected from country, class, community, and even friends and family. But our fundamentalists—by which liberals usually really mean our evangelical and orthodox Christians—are characteristically our least lonely or alienated Americans. They are the ones most likely to be at home with their spouses, children, friends, church, and neighborhood. They also tend to be our most patriotic citizens and are quite devoted to our liberal founding principles, although they do understand those principles somewhat differently than, say, Jefferson or Franklin did.

For orthodox and evangelical religious believers, our liberty is meant to serve free and equal beings living virtuously together under the Creator described in the Bible. They are a little bit puritanical, but every one of our European critics—friendly or otherwise—has noticed that we Americans all are. Our orthodox and evangelical believers are certainly not theocrats or interested in establishing some religion. Our evangelicals, in particular, know that their enthusiasm and what an unfriendly observer might call their consumer

consumer orientation toward worship allows them to flourish in a country where people are free to choose how and what to believe. And they know that a religion that depends on people being born again (and again!) is far from compatible with nostalgia for some imaginary old regime.

Our evangelical believers might be seduced to sending a donation to some slick televangelist or to missionaries aiming to convert Poland to Christianity or even into buying a ticket to a Christian rock concert—usually an offense against both traditional Christianity and classic rock 'n roll. But there is no danger most of them would fall under the thrall of some American Mussolini or a fundamentalist Huey Long. They are much more likely to become devoted to a Ronald Reagan or a George W. Bush and their talk about our nation's God-given mission to defend and promote liberty everywhere. As all our astute European observers have noticed, a distinctive feature of American conservatism is its marginalization of the "radical Right."

We are still threatened by what might loosely be called the fascism of global terrorism. But all the terrorists can really hope to do is to blow lots of us up. (That, of course, is an evil worth working hard to avoid.) Almost nobody believes that Islamic fanaticism is the wave of the future in America, and our young people are not about to be seduced by the religious fanatic's view of the world. We might or might not think that President Bush's confidence that he can bring our liberal principles to bear on the governments of the Middle East is naïve. But if we do, that is only because we think that *they* are not prepared to grasp what *we know* about the truth about human nature, and both our self-proclaimed relativists and our evangelicals share in our perception of this truth. Despite their official relativism, virtually none of our influential professors are open to the extreme Islamic view of, say, the (lack of) rights of women or the near identity of church and state.

We Americans believe, more than ever, that all human beings are equally free and equal individuals; we believe more than ever in the individual's freedom from moral determination by others. Few of us doubt much more than the president that history and technology are on our side. Fatalistic "live for the day" decadence, lots of us think, is for Europeans. They may be immersed in the fantasy that they are living in some posthistorical, postpolitical, postreligious, and postfamilial paradise, but harsh demographic—and, of course, political and economic—realities are, many of us know, going to slap them around soon enough. We driven, optimistic Americans, as David Brooks explains, cannot help but live in the future tense, in hope of the paradise that we will create through our own efforts. Our evangelicals are especially optimistic about what they can do on their own with God's help; their faith actually fuels their self-reliance by showing them that they need not succumb to impersonal forces beyond their control.

The Communists (and Socialists)?

For most of my lifetime, the war against fascism was relegated to World War II movies, and the real war was the Cold War. We conservatives now remember—with some nostalgia—when we all united under President Reagan in defense of human liberty against the evil empire. Some conservatives, in those days, verged on being reactionaries insofar as they believed that—despite the nobility of their cause—history was probably not on their side. Conservatives from Whittaker Chambers to Henry Kissinger believed ours was likely a lost cause. The deepest conservatives in those days—such as Reagan, Thatcher, Solzhenitsyn, Havel, and John Paul II—had confidence that human nature or human liberty and virtue were bound to prevail over every effort to extinguish them through historical reform or revolution. They were so right that all we conservatives today think of ourselves as agreeing with them not only now but then.

It has become a conservative platitude (one with a lot of truth) to say that communism, socialism, and even androgynous feminism—every form of radical social constructionism—has been defeated by human nature. It is certainly a thought we should constantly keep in mind when thinking about the probable future of both human liberty and human virtue. But we can also easily overdo our professions of faith in the power of human nature in the abstract to defeat every form of tyranny. The defeat of communism in the late 1980s also depended on the virtue of the anticommunist dissidents, the statesmanship of Reagan and Thatcher, and even some good luck. There is something contingent about all human accomplishments, and history is never necessarily on anyone's side.

Communism and even socialism are now even less of a threat to liberty and virtue than fascism. Even the threat of the unlimited and degrading progress of the welfare state has diminished considerably. FDR's "liberal"—in the sense of progressive—theory of the welfare state was that government cooperation is a superior method to private competition in solving social problems, and so government gradually grew bigger and better. That vision, his critics charged, marked out the road to serfdom, to the schoolmarmish kinder and gentler despotism that Alexis de Tocqueville feared. There, we would surrender concern for our futures to meddlesome bureaucrats who would surround us with impersonal rules maximizing our security and minimizing our risk. There, virtue in the sense of personal responsibility, charity, or even courage would become superfluous; we would surrender much of our human greatness and misery and lose ourselves in the enjoyment of the present. We would no longer be stuck with virtue. Tocqueville's critique of soft despotism is essential a critique of the indefinite expansion of the nanny state in the direction of socialism and therapeutic, "feel good" pantheism.

Even with the present epidemic of uncontrolled spending—especially on some entitlements, including a new one or two—it is not reasonable to believe that we are slouching toward socialism or soft despotism any more. Nobody, not even in North Korea or Cuba, thinks communism is the wave of the future, and even socialist hopes are on life-support. We can see all too clearly that the scope of the welfare state has certain definite limits. The European social democracies seem destined to fall victim to their birth dearth, and even our relatively minimalist safety net is beginning to face similar problems. Social Security has more than hypothetical actuarial problems, and private and even public pensions seem to have no long-term future. Unions and both employer and employee loyalty are casualties, for better and worse, of the dynamism of the high-tech free market. We cannot explain how we will be able to afford to take care of the growing number of frail, demented, and otherwise "naturally" dependent elderly Americans—Americans who can no longer be productive and are genuinely unfortunate. The irony, of course, is that the plight of many elderly Americans is the result, in part, of the mostly beneficial progress of medical science and technology. More people will be stuck with what we cannot help but think of as the long and degrading dependency of Alzheimer's because of our success in battling heart disease and cancer. The plight of our elderly will also increasingly be due to the corrosion of family ties; the number of single and childless people over sixty-five is growing steadily.

The individual American can count on being more on his own than ever for the foreseeable future. For better and worse, we're going to live in more of an "ownership society" than ever. The virtues of responsible individuals who can secure their future against every contingency will become more especially prized. But let us not fool ourselves into thinking that we will be able to stop hoping to be able to count on the virtues of loyal and loving spouses, children, friends, and lovers—not to mention the completely unearned devotion of caregivers (such as the almost extinct Sisters of Mercy) who serve us without even knowing us—at least as much as we do now. Our longings for self-ownership or autonomy and reliable or loving caregiving will remain in tension with one another, and a somewhat unprecedented kind of virtue will be required to live with that tension well.

The Relativists

Some conservatives have been saying for quite some time that the real enemy of liberty and virtue is not fascism or communism or progressivism but relativism. We often associate that attack on relativism with thinkers who believe we live "after virtue," or without a "coherent narrative" that gives us a persuasive account of those moral goods human beings share in common. The result is that we believe that one "value system" is finally as good as another. More precisely, we tend to believe that all values are merely subjective or private—mere preferences that cannot be judged according to standards of truth and falsity or good and evil.

Relativism is sometimes defended as a way of defending non-Western ways of life from the wrecking balls of globalization and universalism. Just because we have *more* money, power, and freedom than they *do*, does not mean that we are *better* than they *are*. As sensible as that statement may be, our relativists usually do not believe it: Their real opinion is that nonrelativists are inferior to relativists with respect to both truth and virtue. All non-Western ways of life tend to be judgmental and therefore tyrannical when it comes to certain fundamental human choices—such as who to have sex with and why. Only sophisticated, Western relativists can curb our instinct toward moralism with the *Seinfeld* phrase "not that there's anything wrong with that" and really, really mean it. And only we can be so moralistic about our nonjudgmentalism. Our relativism is mainly a tool in the service of egalitarian individualism; it levels all distinctions that privilege one human being or group of human beings over others. Virtually none of our intellectuals is relativistic, for example, when it comes to opinions about race, class, gender, or even sexual orientation. A professor, even at an evangelical college, would (with good reason) be fired for dividing his class up into small groups to prepare for a debate on the strengths and weaknesses of racism, and the same will become increasingly true even about same-sex marriage.

But it is still true that our high-tech relativism tends toward nihilism (not that there is anything necessarily wrong with that). We modern human beings tend to identify reality with whatever we can control, with what we can manipulate rationally with our freedom and security in mind. We tend to identify reality with technology, with practically effective science. So we tend to identify real education with productivity, with what teaches us to generate wealth and power. Anything that is not technological is not real; it is a mere whim or preference or "value." So we can use phrases like "sexual preference" without smirking, as if choosing to have sex is like choosing dessert, and we celebrate our technological success with little reservation about indefinitely expanding our menu of free choice.

Choices concerning wisdom and beauty, love and death, friendship and virtue, and God and country are all mere preferences that cannot be judged according to the standard of truth or reality. They are, from a technological view, smoke that weighs nothing. That means we cannot expect to use our nontechnological "values" to control and direct technological development. How can you really control something—technology—with nothing, or preferences then are nothing more than preferences? So techno-relativism or nihilism imprisons us to the unlimited development of technology. Technology so understood makes virtue impossible by abolishing the real distinction between virtue and vice.

Nobody can deny that sophisticated Americans often talk and act as if techno-relativism or high-tech nihilism as I just described is true. They combine a nice, laidback, apathetic indifference to traditional moral distinctions with an increasingly paranoid, puritanical, and prohibitionist attitude toward health and safety. They demand that sex be, as far as possible, "safe sex," or disconnected altogether from the risky business of birth and death, and they do what they can to be productive or as technologically effective as possible to secure themselves from the ravages of nature and bad luck. Otherwise, they speak the gentle, therapeutic language of nonjudgmentalism and the inalienable right to self-esteem. Despite their libertarianism when it comes to abortion or same-sex marriage, they are all for a bigger, more intrusive government when it comes to the dangers of second-hand smoke or driving without a seatbelt or getting supersized or the trans-fatty culture of death of the Oreo cookie. And they are obsessed with fending off every new "risk factor" through the most scientific forms of diet and exercise. Disease, debility, destitution, dependency, and death are real evils to be avoided; everything else is a matter of taste. What remains of virtue, according to this technological view, is the real responsibility embodied in personal fitness and personal, careerist productivity. What remains of vice, conversely, is obesity, smoking, and, more generally, bohemian or spiritual indifference to the bottom line.

Some of our conservative anti-relativists, such as Allan Bloom, have held that this relativistic talk and survivalist behavior provide evidence that sophisticated Americans have become flat-souled, that they have surrendered somehow their distinctively human longings, that they are no longer moved by love and death. They are clever, competent specialists, but they are no longer fit to be philosophers or poets or theologians. And they are virtually incapable, as the novelist Tom Wolfe complains, of practicing the stoic virtue of proud, serene indifference to fluctuations in fortune, or the martial virtue of courage in the face of death. They have lapsed into something like what Tocqueville calls apathetic individualism, unmoved by the heart-enlarging passions that connect them to large families, lots of friends, country, God, or the truth.

Sophisticated Americans, from this view, are becoming more and more like the characters portrayed on *Seinfeld*, a show about nothing. Or for that matter, the characters we saw on *Friends*, where for most of the show's history the characters were incapable of either marrying and procreating with each other (much less understanding themselves as citizens or creatures) or making new and enduring friendships outside their small and boring group. But let us not go too far in identifying shows about nothing with human reality. Very few of us inhabit the worlds portrayed on *Friends, Seinfeld,* or *Curb Your Enthusiasm,* where people seem to have plenty of everything with very little work and even less virtue.

Our relativism really is in some measure connected with a drift toward apathetic individualism. Educated people may well be both nicer—which is not the same thing as saying they have better manners—and more self-centered than ever. But Tocqueville was still wrong to believe that Americans end up surrendering concern for their own, individual futures. It is certainly not true that sophisticated Americans today are not moved by the prospect of their own deaths. Techno-relativism or nihilism, in fact, has the tendency to turn individuals into control freaks. People experience their existences as more contingent and more dependent on their own efforts than ever.

People have become more paranoid about themselves and their own. They have fewer children than ever in part because they are more self-centered, but also in part because they perceive parenthood as more difficult than ever. Our planned parenthoods leave the having and rearing of children less to chance than ever before. When parents left the number of children they had up to chance, they, without ever having made that choice, were sometimes stuck with what seems to us the exceedingly arduous and dangerous venture of taking care of a large family. Very, very few sophisticated parents—and almost none who are not pretty religious—today make the choice to take that chance. The risk is far too great: parents now think they have to secure their children's future all alone in a fundamentally hostile environment.

Everyone knows that the more children people have, the more laidback they get about parenting. There is even a sound sociobiological explanation for that fact: The more kids you have, the more likely it is that your genes will get to the next generation, as nature intends. The one-kid strategy will always subject gene perpetuation too much to chance for parents ever really to relax. And virtues like courage make little sense if everything depends on one's own survival. Today's sophisticated kids are both overprotected and overachieving; life is at once too easy and too hard for the virtues associated, say, with love and friendship to flourish.

Relativism and Biotechnology

We conservatives notice that our experts' therapeutic words do not really correspond to our hard lives; we cannot, in fact, talk love, death, the soul, and the need for hard work and virtue out of existence. Some conservatives, such as Leon Kass and Francis Fukuyama, fear that this contradiction might be resolved by biotechnology. Through our pursuit of "ageless" or indefinitely long lives, we might surrender the most intimate details of our lives to technological determination, separate sex from procreation altogether, and turn reproduction into manufacturing. We might also be compelled to submit to genetic enhancements that will transform our very being.

With some sort of very reliable super-Prozac we might be able to rid ourselves of our anxious sense of contingency; we might be able to engineer moods that will maximize our happiness, health, and productivity. Bad. alienating, unproductive moods will become diseases to be cured; loneliness has already become "social phobia." Biotechnology might bring into being Tocqueville's soft despotism or a kinder, gentler version of the Brave New World. The fear is that biotechnological progress will finally allow us to surrender our liberty for our security. The thought that human nature always defeats human history might become progressively more irrelevant as we figure out ways to change our very natures. Androgyny, for example, is ridiculous as a project for social reform, unless it can be biologically engineered into existence. The most thoughtful and extreme feminists know that women will only be completely liberated when biotechnology can be used to turn reproduction into a purely artificial or mechanical process; only the use of artificial wombs can free women from the natural slavery having babies imposes on them alone.

Biotechnology combined with techno-relativism does have tyrannical potential. Our present reproductive freedom that we have won through pro-choice positions on contraception and abortion might have to give way to a new pro-life legal regimen. It will be just too dangerous to have too many genetically unenhanced—or comparatively stupid and disease-ridden—Catholic, Evangelical, and Mormon kids running around. It will also be too dangerous and burdensome to us all not to abort babies with significant genetic defects that cannot be fixed.

And if mood control becomes reliable, it may well become a condition of employment: If moods, as the technological relativist believes, are merely collections of chemicals to be altered at will, we will have no reason not to be in the best possible mood for the line of work we have chosen. Techno-relativism deprives us of any point of view that would allow us to resist such biotechnological determination. It would be ridiculous to believe, for example, that our moods open us to the truth about our being, that anxiety and loneliness, in particular, may not be just pathologies caused by contemporary social forces or correctible chemical imbalances, but rather indispensable clues to who we really are. Techno-relativists cannot claim an inalienable right to their moods. But this right may still be natural: One response to all our efforts at therapeutic mood control is anger, the mood that more and more drives our most popular music.

Still, we actually have plenty of reasons to believe that the fears of Kass and Fukuyama—like those of Tocqueville and Nietzsche—concerning the "dehumanizing" effects of biotechnology are greatly exaggerated. If mood control meant obliterating our self-consciousness and making us into contented chimps, maybe it would be possible. But most or all of us, in our pride, would not consent to such treatment, and even if our scientists attempted to reduce most of us to mere bodies, they would, in their pride, exempt themselves. We really want to be able to fine-tune our moods with a variety of conflicting human goals in mind.

We want just the right amount and right kind of self-consciousness. We want to be happy, but not to be too happily or mindlessly content. We want our happiness to be human, and we know that human happiness is both more intense and less pure than animal contentment. We want to be alienated enough to be creative and productive. We know that we do not want to live without any art and music at all, and a flat-souled technician is no audience for Shakespeare or Mozart or Johnny Cash or even John Lennon's incoherent imaginings. If we got too happy in the present through virtual technology, then we would languish as consumers of real technology, and our progress toward ever greater wealth, power, security, and freedom would slow to a crawl. Our free market would lose the psychological foundation of the dynamism that fuels its progress. We would remain way too vulnerable to disease, weather, terrorists, the Chinese, and the asteroids that always threaten to pulverize our planet. We cannot let our virtual happiness cause us to end up really dead! Studies show, after all, that bad moods predict the future better than good ones.

The least we can say is that the power to design our moods will end up heightening our anxious sense of contingency in some ways, even as it may alleviate it in others. We conservatives can see that biotechnological enthusiasts overpromise when they suggest that we will soon be able to reliably feel good without being good. The need for virtue will not fade away, but partially successful efforts at the biotechnological reconstruction of our souls do promise to leave us chaotic or confused enough to make the practice of virtue more difficult than ever. The truth is that we do not understand ourselves (at least by ourselves) well enough to be able to figure out the best possible mixture of moody qualities that would be the ideal soul; we characteristically lack the virtue—the courage—to think clearly about how the good stuff (like love, truth, deserved pride, or "self-esteem" and all that) depends on the bad stuff (like anxiety, dependence, and death). Even if moods and our other soulful qualities became chemical silly putty in our hands, we still would not know with any certainty what to do.

The impulse to biotechnology itself is another indication that Tocqueville was wrong about our human future: He feared that the modern version of the dogma of materialism might become a self-fulfilling prophecy. For someone who understands himself as nothing but a free individual, nothing existed until he came into existence, and when he is gone, all is gone. In other words, existence, meaning my living body, is but a moment—a moment I work to make last as long as possible—between two abysses. Believing too well that everything dies when I die, I will not work to create anything that lives beyond my biological existence. Nothing will be built or written with the intention of passing the test of time, because I myself (and thus *being* itself) will not pass the test of time. There will be no resistance to the technological imperative of planned obsolescence, and eventually we will stop living for or even having the children that nature intends to replace us. The result will be devastating for truth, beauty, and virtue, to say nothing about the effect on the species. To be human, Tocqueville thought, is to be moved to thought and action by one's longing for eternity or immortality, and believing too well that that longing cannot be satisfied will (Tocqueville sometimes feared) cause our humanity to wither away.

The truth is we are working to replace natural evolution with biotechnological or conscious and volitional evolution precisely because we remain dissatisfied with the limits of our biological existence. We are working to push death back so far that we individuals will experience our lives as indefinitely long. We will not literally become immortal, because we will never transcend altogether our dependence on bodies or matter. But perhaps our lives can become so long that we will literally be unable to count their days, and so we will no longer be haunted by death or the miserable experience of the contingency of our own existence in an indifferent or hostile universe. No longer defined by death, we will be truly free to choose to be defined by something better. Most of our understanding of virtue has been making the best of a bad situation, but why could not virtue become making the best of a much better situation? Biotechnology puts an optimistic face on our materialism; it need not culminate in the existentialist's or stoic's fatalism about his future. What is material we can comprehend; what we can comprehend we can control—or manipulate or transform with our individual longings in mind.

But the psychology of biotechnological optimism is as flawed as the pessimism of end-of-history or Brave New World thought. The more we freely push back natural necessity, the more contingent or accidental the perception of our existence becomes. The more our very being depends upon our hard work, the less necessary death seems, the more accidental it seems. Accidental death will remain possible, and it will seem more terrible than death in the past. Consider, for example, that the great progress we have made in eradicating death in childhood has probably made us more paranoid than ever about our children's security. Virtues such as courage that help us live well with what we really know about ourselves make sense if we know we have to go sometime—

sometime rather soon—anyway, but they are insanity if we know there is no reason that we have to go any time in particular. The pursuit of immortal glory makes sense if that is the best immortal deal we can get, but I will not care whether or not my name lives on indefinitely if I can literally live on indefinitely instead. To paraphrase the great Woody Allen: The immortality I hope my work wins me is just not as good as the immortality that comes through not dying. The more trustworthy and less wimpy St. Augustine made exactly the same point.

The prospect of indefinite longevity will not extinguish our anxious sense of contingency. That does not mean that indefinite longevity should either be resisted or embraced in the name of virtue, dignity, and happiness. If we have the technological capacity to achieve it, we will achieve it, and even the Bible says there is nothing wrong with being able to live a long, long time. Our happiness and dignity will still continue to depend on having virtues other than the survivalist ones, and techno-relativism will remain untrue.

Darwinian Conservatism

The two leading sources of opposition to techno-relativism in our country are Darwin and the Bible. Their common enemy can also be called radical libertarianism, or the view that we are free from nature and God to design or construct our lives however we please. The political scientist Larry Arnhart writes provocatively in favor of "Darwinian conservatism," and he is joined by Francis Fukuyama, James Q. Wilson, and Steven Rhoads, among others. Darwinianism means to be the antidote to relativism by showing that nature gives us definite guidance on how to live happily and purposefully. We have been given social instincts that are reliable foundations for virtue. Men and women have been given different natural purposes, and those purposes, of course, are complementary. We are happy when we follow nature's guidance by marrying, having children, raising them responsibly, and generally being involved in social and political life. We can see that women seduced by the feminist or liberationist view that they are no different from men are often stuck with frustrated lives because they denied their natural, feminine desires for marriage and children. And we can also see how miserable self-destructive men often become when they are deprived of the civilizing or domesticating influence of wives and children. The Darwinian conservatives teach us that what is often called "traditional" morality is often better called "natural" morality.

Darwinian sociobiology also shows us why we have a natural preference for those close to us, and therefore why laws protecting private property reflect the truth about our natures. The abstract extremes of communism and atomistic individualism have no real or natural foundation; neither do existentialism or creationism. Religion has limited utility as a reinforcement for our social duties and as a way of providing the communal comfort for which we crave, but it becomes perverse when it teaches us to be dissatisfied with ourselves as natural or biological beings.

The Darwinians are surely right that we sacrifice some moral orientation and happiness when we distance ourselves too much from the natural purposes we share in some way with the other animals. People from big families surely are usually happier than people from small ones, and certainly happier than the lonely people who have no family ties at all. And the attempt to reconstruct all our instinctual or loving and friendly ties with others in terms of contract and consent is a recipe for misery. The Darwinians can help to explain why radical social constructionism of both the libertarian and the communist varieties—the various attempts to replace the natural world too completely with a "designer" world of our making—are both contrary to and tend to be defeated by human nature. The disastrous social policies of the 1960s were responsible for the increase in pathologies such as crime, divorce, and single- parent families, and conservatives can usefully employ sociobiological arguments to defend traditional morality against every form of cultural liberationism. Sociobiologists should, if they have any guts, have a lot to say about the naturalness of same-sex marriage.

The Darwinian conservatives, though, have trouble explaining the intensity of modern technological and biotechnological efforts to conquer nature. Some Darwinian conservatives say that we should not worry about biotechnology too much; its use will be guided by the purposes we have been given by nature. But can evolved nature really be the source of our desire to push back death indefinitely, of our refusal to submit to a definite lifespan and step aside for our replacements? Can Darwinian sociobiology really explain why the wealthy, powerful, and free Europeans—healthy animals living in good environments—have more or less chosen to stop having children? The Darwinian conservative Friedrich von Hayek predicted that the triumph of the free market over socialism would be the source of a rising birthrate. He was wrong; after communism fell the birth rate continued to fall in Europe as well as in the sophisticated or secular parts of our country and it is now below the replacement level.

The Darwinian cannot explain why one species and one species alone has become smart enough to know the truth about evolved nature or sociobiology, or why that knowledge has had such a perverse effect on that species. Our country, from one view, is divided into two sizeable factions on evolution— those who claim that Darwin more or less teaches the truth about our nature and destiny, and those who think he does not. The latter group, of course, is largely composed of evangelical and orthodox observant believers. Those who believe Darwin teaches the truth increasingly do not live as evolution seems to intend. They are living for themselves, and not for their children or for the future of their species. Those believers who live in Darwin denial tend to be perfect pictures of evolutionary health. They are marrying, having lots of children, raising them well, and not so unwillingly stepping aside for them as nature or God intends.

Those who say they believe that, as products of evolution, we are as at home in the world as every other animal tend to live particularly homeless, rootless, alienated, very individualistic lives. Those who say that the natural world is not really our true home are more at home with their natural inclinations and limitations. It would seem that the scientists most interested in giving our species every evolutionary advantage or perhaps even an evolutionary future should insist that the theory of evolution not be taught in our public schools. Those who do not believe in that theory's comprehensive truth clearly have an evolutionary advantage over those who do. Any good Darwinian has to admit that what the Mormons believe is better for the survival and flourishing of our species than what the sociobiologists believe.

The Darwinian conservatives cannot really convince free individuals why they should rest content with the view of nature the Darwinian sociobiologists describe. Evolution is blind and pitiless, caring not at all for individuals and only for species. The goal of natural selection, of course, is not the flourishing or perpetuation of particular organisms, including human ones. Anyone who sees all that is implied in that truth would immediately begin to work hard to change it, and the opinion that it could not be changed would not lead to the grateful acceptance of natural guidance but to fatalistic existentialism. We are the species full of individuals who think that they can know that all existence is a purposeless accident. The human individual, in truth, is not at home in the natural world, and his free and rational behavior is in many ways a mysterious exception to the laws of nature that govern all the other species. Apparently the being smart enough to know the truth of sociobiology or evolutionary psychology is too smart, too unhappy, and too screwed up to let that truth remain completely true.

Evolutionary theory, of course, must account for human goods such as love, friendship, and virtue in terms of the survival and flourishing of the species. The social behaviors that evolution may have woven into the very fabric of our natures are not intended by nature to be good for *me*. They are meant to turn *me* into effective species-perpetuation fodder. That fact should make us modern individuals even more suspicious of love or friendship— or listening to our social instincts in general—than we already are. We are increasingly refusing to lose our minds in service to family, God, and country, and the species, of course, inspires less devotion still. No Darwinian ever claims that any animal actually *cares* about the future of its species, and there is no evolutionary reason to believe that the animal that comes to know that he or she merely exists for the species would, as a result, care about the species more. Individualistic philosophers—such as Hobbes and Locke—might justly be criticized for reducing human motivation and human virtue to what is best for the individual's biological survival. But their teaching better addresses the longing of real human beings than does Darwinian evolution. If we are stuck with choosing between views of the world whose bottom lines are species survivalism and individual survivalism, there is really no contest.

Our sophisticated Americans, in truth, are almost always libertarian sociobiologists; they say, seemingly quite incoherently, both that we are autonomous and that we are not different in kind from the other species. Nobody speaks of autonomous chimps or chimp biotechnology or chimp poetry. But Darwinian libertarianism may make more sense than it first seems. Properly understood, our understanding of ourselves as free individuals depends on a Darwinian understanding of nature, and ourselves as emergent exceptions to what is otherwise true about nature. Traditional societies see themselves in terms of descent from the gods and heroic ancestors, and even we progressive Americans are capable of seeing ourselves as having fallen away from the wisdom and virtue of our founders. Darwinians see themselves as having ascended from the slime and the chimps, with the implication, of course, that our ascent is in the direction of divinity. The more we progress, the less dependent we are on nature, and the more we are, like God, governed by our own wills and intelligence. The image of evolutionary ascent is not a conservative one, and we cannot purge that image from our view of evolution.

Some Darwinians say that the evolutionary theory's "Great Demotion" of human beings to nothing but clever chimps should make us humble: No longer are we deluded by the vain idea that we are made in the image of God. But surely that idea is less vain than the belief that we can comprehend all that exists according to a single materialistic theory, and we cannot help but add the still more arrogant technological thought that what we can understand we can eventually control (or what we can control we can eventually understand). Over time and through our hard work, we become less like the chimps and more like the gods. Everything natural is merely transitional, and perhaps nature itself might have no permanent hold on beings that have evolved enough to be able to take charge of their own evolution. The promise of evolution is, finally, that we are moving away from being determined by nature to determining what we are for ourselves, that we are moving toward achieving personal control over our biological lives, that we need not remain forever slaves of natural or bodily processes.

The idea of evolution as ascent allows us to see death itself as nothing permanent, but as a kind of contingent biological event that can, like everything else, evolve out of existence. Our individual experience of ourselves as contingent and temporary beings may itself be temporary, as we reasonably change the goal of evolution from species to individual survival. The existence of the species, after all, is as contingent as any other evolutionary product; it is the accidental result of a process that might just as easily have turned out differently. Nature, finally, gives us no reason at all to privilege the species over the individual.

The idea of evolution suggests that human intelligence will eventually outwit the impersonal intelligence of biological evolution. Human intelligence and consciousness may have been the accidental products of biological evolution, but we human beings have already shown we can bring mindless natural forces under our conscious control. Because the idea of evolution cannot help but be rife with "speciesism" or opposed to species relativism, it really does not offer much opposition to the techno-relativism characteristic of our species alone. Its deepest tendency, contrary to the intention of the Darwinian conservatives, is to undermine virtue based on the acceptance of the intractable limitations of human nature or the human condition.

Biblical Conservatives

Our evangelicals are opposed to both the Darwinian view of reality and techno-relativism, seeing, more or less correctly, their interdependence. Evangelicals object to the dogmatic atheism of the theory of evolution. They sometimes object, too simply, that its materialism reduces human beings to beings without souls or spiritual openness to God. They also object, with more reason, that it reduces human beings to meaningless, hopeless accidents devoid of direction. Evolution, of course, treats all species that way, but only members of our species can both know that truth about nature and naturally crave purpose and direction. Our evangelicals rightly notice that the theory of evolution does not teach its proponents humility. Evolutionists proudly think that they can explain and do everything and be happy without God. The true experience of humility is of our ineradicable dependence on God for our very being. All virtue depends on humble gratitude for what the Creator has given us and our truthful acceptance of our inability to free ourselves from our experiences of contingency or homelessness without faith. And all virtue depends on our consciousness of and responsibility for our flaws, our sins, which cannot be overcome by either thought, work, or in any other way on our own.

Evangelicals are sometimes attracted to theories such as "intelligent design" which explicitly point toward a Designer or a Creator. But usually all they really want to do is oppose the dogmatic conclusion that what we know through science demonstrates that the world could not have been created, and so they are mainly interested in the proponents of intelligent design's often quite intelligent and effective exposure of problems in attempts to use the homogeneous theory of evolution to account for everything. Our evangelicals often teach that if it were not for the absolute truth promulgated by the word of God in the Bible, then relativism would be true. Only the Bible and God's grace, and not nature, provides us the guidance we need. Certainly it could not be true that we were born to be autonomous or merely self-determining beings, to create freely our own purposes out of nothing. Some dependence and trust is required for us to think and act well, and the modern individual who experiences love only as a source of unreliable dependence and subjection is unable to do either. The fundamental insight of those who hold that the world was created is that our loving, dutiful dependence is not only inevitable but good.

For even those who do not believe in biblical revelation, evangelical psychology might have the merit of explaining why we are stuck with virtue: We, thank God, do not have in our power the ability to make ourselves more or less than human, or to engineer a world in which we will be either completely homeless or completely at home, or one in which we will simply be happy or unendurably and hopelessly miserable. Being human, as the Bible says, means being born to trouble. The moral and spiritual conflicts or at least tensions that constitute the human soul are not problems to be solved, but just part of our being. That is why we are stuck with virtue to live well with what we really know. Our techno-relativism has not flattened our souls but disoriented them; we are miserable in the absence of any sense of God or the good to orient our lives. Our longings for love and friendship, God and immortality, cannot help but trouble us, but we can make the mistake of denying their real existence or regarding them as merely legacies of our oppression. Those desires and longings persist whatever we say or do, and the Christian psychologist Pascal never tired of explaining that staying in trouble and never really at home gives us plenty of reason not to despair. There are many reasons we should be grateful for being stuck with living morally demanding lives.

The conservative Darwinians are wrong to think that our basic social institutions such as marriage and the family can be solidly rooted in natural moral instinct alone, and the individualists or libertarians are wrong that they can have any sort of future if completely reconstructed according to the liberal principles of calculation, consent, and contract. They are distorted if we attempt to understand them without a sacred dimension that points beyond the biological existence of any particular individual or even of the species in the direction of God, and the loving loyalty and other duties they impose upon us cannot be chosen against without ungratefully denying the truth about our very being.

If the demographic crisis (which is closely connected in Europe to a decline in work ethic) in the sophisticated West is due mostly to excessive secularization, as seems likely, it would seem that we liberal conservatives are right not to ignore the fact that even the future of our species depends on the future of God. Or more precisely, the future of our species will be in those societies where God has a future. The future of liberal societies would seem to depend on God and virtue not being reduced to useful supports to individual liberty, and the future of America would depend on our evangelicals, orthodox believers, Mormons, and so forth continuing to believe in a most unironic way that ours is a nation under God.

The philosopher Heidegger called the growth of the tendency of people to live in the thrall of the wholly technological view of reality "Americanization." And at first glance it is easy to see why that name makes sense: Compared to old Europe we do seem short on roots, tradition, culture and all that, although for a European today cultivation often means having a leisurely glass of wine in a square outside a cathedral that they themselves could never become imaginative or devoted enough either to rebuild or even attend. Our dominant form of religion seems too vulgar, enthusiastic, and traditionless to resist domination by some combination of high technology and therapeutic psychology. Our evangelicals, it is true enough, grab on to every technological advance that comes along to spread the Word, and they are mighty naïve about how the medium might compromise the message. We also have to admit that too often touchy-feely psychology replaces theology in Evangelical Sunday Schools. But the evidence shows that their critics, both American and European, exaggerate greatly the extent to which our evangelicals—not to mention our other observant believers—here succumbed to techno-relativism.

From what I have seen, evangelicals are taught quite clearly that pragmatism, relativism, and indefinite moral freedom are anti-biblical. Human beings are bound by the absolute truth of God's revelation, and they are given very definite and demanding duties as parents, spouses, creatures, and citizens. The evangelical God is personal and loving, but also quite judgmental. From the perspective of a traditional Catholic or an Orthodox Jew, evangelicals inhabit a perhaps unstable but real place between orthodoxy and individualism. In addition to their admirable family lives—which are inexplicable without taking virtue seriously—we can call attention to European perplexity over our evangelical and orthodox voting behavior.

Our European critics often criticize us Americans for, in effect, not being Americanized enough in Heidegger's sense. In 2004, they called our "moral values" or, better, virtue voters stupid for not voting on merely technical grounds—for the party that would do best in delivering health care, social security, more secure alliances, and so forth. They could not believe that Americans really regarded human nature and biblical revelation as the real foundation of issues such as abortion, same-sex marriage, and biotechnology. But our virtue voters might respond that because of our faith, our lives are more real than those of Europeans living in some fantasy about a postfamilial, postreligious, and postpolitical paradise that they have created for themselves. The result is that our country has more of a real future.

The weakness of our biblical conservatism—especially our evangelical conservatism—is its characteristic view that if it were not for the absolute truth of biblical revelation relativism would be true. Their perception that America is now in the midst of a "culture war" between biblical and secular "worldviews" concedes far too much to their opponents. If their perception is true, after all, they are probably destined to lose that war. Given our separation of church and state, we would have to conclude that what is common to all Americans is the "secular" view of the truth of techno-relativism or promiscuous nonjudgmentalism on everything but individual health and safety. That common, "rational" view would have to dominate our public life, and the countercultural, biblical view would be no more than a private preference or taste.

But the truth is that even if biblical revelation did not exist both our sociobiologists and our libertarians or techno-relativists would be far from completely right about what human beings are. Darwinian conservatives are right that our evangelical conservatives need to give arguments about the foundation of virtue in human nature that all their fellow citizens can appreciate. The natural human good that is the family, for example, can be defended without recourse to the Bible, and the evangelicals' opponents— above all those who disconnect rights from virtue—have to be made to defend themselves against the charge that rights can only be good if they are compatible with the social, familial, political, and religious virtues that make life worth living. But the evangelicals also join the libertarians insofar as they see that the truth about human freedom cannot be captured by some materialistic theory or a merely natural or civil theology. We are free by nature in a way the other animals are not—not only to secure our own self-preservation but to know God and the good; our natural longings point beyond themselves in the direction of God. No genuinely natural account of the human person could reduce all of his greatness and misery to either individual- or species-survivalist behavior.

An account of the whole truth about human beings as they actually exist would incorporate both the partial truth about our freedom reflected in the theory of the autonomous individual and the partial truth about our natural sociality we see reflected in the extremely clever and friendly chimp described by the sociobiologists. But it would also have to include humans' loving openness to the truth about all things, including ourselves, our incurable longing for God, and our somewhat mysterious but quite real capability to have the virtue—which includes some combination of proud magnanimity and a humble and grateful acceptance of dependence—to live well with what we really know. Our distinctive excellences, troubles, flaws, and perversities have a natural foundation in the gift of language given to our species alone. Our religious conservatives—for the benefit of truth, virtue, and the future of our political life—must therefore reinvigorate the more comprehensive understanding of human nature found in the great tradition of natural law, of which our Declaration of Independence can be understood as a part.

Epilogue

The Enduring Reagan

William Kristol

WHAT LESSONS SHOULD CONSERVATIVES learn from Ronald Reagan's legacy? I went to Washington to work for President Reagan and was one of those very low-level foot soldiers in the "Reagan Revolution." We all defined ourselves as "Reaganites," as participants in the "Reagan Revolution." We were extremely proud to be working, even though many levels removed, from the president himself; and it is with that background that I would like, in this essay, to address the significance of his career and his presidency.

It is not unwise to begin by focusing on conservatism as a movement, because Reagan came out of that movement. If Reagan succeeded, the movement and its various incarnations, and its various strands, certainly deserve a good deal of credit for the success that he achieved.

Counterintuitive Leadership

While working for Reagan in 1975 and 1976 during his failed primary challenge against President Gerald Ford, Jeff Bell, an impressive Washington political commentator, gained some profound insights into Reagan's unique leadership style. Bell recounts a humorous story about campaign manager John Sears and his frustration with Reagan's unwillingness to study the briefing books that were prepared for him before his television appearances and debates with Ford. Reagan studied some, but not in the way suggested by Sears, who wanted Reagan to commit to memory numerous policy details. This made Sears furious at times, but Reagan knew instinctively where he stood on the grand issues of the day, and he was confident that his core beliefs would successfully guide him in his particular responses. And when it came to actually making a policy decision or even a political assessment, Reagan almost always proved to possess uncannily good judgment.

Reagan was often at odds with his fellow conservatives, according to Bell. This was partly the result of the usual political rivalries and policy disagreements that arise in a political campaign. Yet the major reason for this state of affairs was that Reagan, more than any other politician up to that time, had developed a coherent worldview by immersing himself in the conservative writings and journals of the day, such as *National Review, Human Events*, the *Wall Street Journal* editorial page, and serious foreign policy books. As a result, Reagan internalized this information in a way that allowed him to trust his instincts and make good calls on the fly, the way you must in a presidential campaign or inside the Oval Office.

In a way, that is the real-world test of a political movement or set of political ideas: do they provide guidance for making key judgments on a wide variety of issues? Reagan's judgment was almost always accurate and often far-seeing, a testament to his practical political wisdom.

The Courage to Make History

When reflecting upon Reagan's remarkable political career, the primary attributes that come to mind are his unflinching courage and individual conviction. Reagan was a truly courageous political leader, something that we sometimes forget in the glow of Reagan's rehabilitation by even some in today's mainstream media. It is now the popular understanding, with the benefit of hindsight, that Reagan was a successful president, especially given his aggressive defense and foreign policy initiatives that spelled the doom of the Soviet empire. We now write, after the fact, a narrative in which this was inevitable or at least not a big surprise. After all, he was a great communicator, and he had terrific charisma.

So why should we be surprised that Reagan became what he became? At the time, of course, it did not seem preordained at all. Actually, what is quite striking to anyone who reads a little history of Reagan's career is how bold he was in his choices and how much courage he demonstrated in standing up against conventional wisdom, not only of the political punditry of his time, but even, at times, of his many conservative allies and advisors.

Greek philosophy and the Hebrew Bible disagree on a lot of matters, but to some extent they do agree on the value of courage. Aristotle said that courage is the first of the virtues because without it, you cannot really practice the others. Similarly, the Hebrew Bible notes, when recounting the death of Moses (a real moment of crisis for the Jewish people) that the first thing God told Joshua was "to be strong and courageous." Courage, then, appears to be the cardinal virtue, not only for politics, but for all aspects of human relations.

In terms of Reagan's courage, he began his national political career audaciously (and some said foolishly) in October 1964, volunteering to give a speech on national television for Barry Goldwater as that campaign plummeted toward one of the greatest defeats in American political history. Most of Reagan's California cabinet of advisors, as well as people who wished him well, counseled him not to give that speech. According to their reasoning, Reagan had a promising political career; why should he risk that in introducing himself to the American people by speaking on national television for a candidate who appeared headed to certain defeat? At that time, 60 percent of the American people thought that Goldwater was a deranged extremist, a perception that LBJ's advertisements tried to reinforce by linking Goldwater to nuclear Armageddon. Suffice it to say, then, that giving a speech for Goldwater went against most of the conventional wisdom of the day. Nevertheless, Reagan believed in Goldwater, and more importantly, he believed in the principles of limited government that animated Goldwater's campaign. Consequently, Reagan went ahead and made the speech, and though it did not prevent Goldwater from going down to ignominious defeat, it did prove to be a widely popular speech with an unprecedented grassroots reaction. This bold action, informed by principle and executed with courage, helped lay the groundwork for Reagan's own successful run for California governor in 1966.

We also tend to forget that when Ronald Reagan ran for governor of California, he first faced a primary fight against a popular mainstream Republican mayor, George Christopher of San Francisco, who was considered the favorite, especially among California's Republican establishment. On paper, Reagan's credentials appeared meager: he had never held elective office, and was now associated with the losing Goldwater wing of the GOP. Clearly, there were less risky ways to launch your political career than by challenging a popular incumbent mayor and trumpeting your conservative values. Yet despite all of that, Reagan defied the odds in 1966, beating Christopher in the primary and then going on to defeat the incumbent governor, Democrat Pat Brown, who just four years earlier had (seemingly) knocked out Richard Nixon permanently from electoral politics. This began a pattern for Reagan: defying the political odds through an unapologetic assertion of conservative political principles.

With his unlikely victory, Reagan immediately considered challenging Nixon in 1968 for the Republican presidential nomination, but he chose wisely instead to serve two strong terms as governor of California, establishing an impressive record of effective conservative governance that would serve him well in his subsequent runs for the presidency. In 1975, when the Republican Party was reeling after Watergate and Nixon's resignation, Gerald Ford attempted to pull the party together, and at first, Reagan obliged. Eventually, however, Reagan decided that he simply had too many deep disagreements with the Nixon-Ford brand of Republicanism on a number of important issues, most notably détente with the Soviet Union, which he viewed as appeasement and ultimately counterproductive to long-term American security. Instead, Reagan supported initiatives that challenged directly Soviet hegemony, which he hoped would one day lead to the ultimate defeat of the Soviet Union, not merely coexistence with the evil empire.

So in another bold move, Reagan decided to take on the national Republican establishment and oppose President Ford in the 1976 GOP primaries. By challenging a sitting president, Reagan assured himself of practically zero political support among members of Congress, fellow governors, and GOP professionals. As expected, almost the entire Republican establishment fell in line with Ford, which made it very difficult for Reagan to mount a serious campaign in the early primary states. Although the New Hampshire primary was closer than expected, Reagan proceeded to lose the first nine primary contests to Ford. At that juncture, his advisors wanted him to pull out of the race to generate at least a modicum of good will, and most of all, unity, within the party. But a few stalwart supporters, most notably first-term North Carolina senator Jesse Helms, talked Reagan into making the Tar Heel state his last stand, and making foreign policy the central issue of his campaign. The Reagan campaign bought a half hour of television time in the state, which Reagan used to condemn the Salt II Treaty. After posting an upset victory in North Carolina, Reagan went on to win the bulk of the remaining primaries, coming only a few votes short of securing a majority of delegates at the 1976 GOP convention. And at that convention, Reagan, who was not expected to speak, gave a very moving impromptu concession speech and endorsement of Ford, after the president himself had called Reagan up to the rostrum. The speech actually became a rallying cry to the Republican Party, not only in 1976, when Ford almost made a miraculous comeback against challenger Jimmy Carter, but also in 1980, when Reagan finally became the standard-bearer for his party.

Today, when we think of Reagan, we see one of the finest presidents of the twentieth century, someone almost preordained for greatness. But as I have tried to point out, we tend to forget the entrepreneurship, the risk-taking, and the courage that he demonstrated throughout his political career. He always fought for what he thought was right, frequently ignoring the short-term tactical calculations of advisors and the current conventional wisdom. It is worth remembering that the most consequential American president in the last half-century was someone who rarely followed the safe and easy course throughout his career. Indeed, Reagan's rise to political prominence is a profile in courage and fortitude.

The Indispensable Reagan

This chronicling of Reagan's courage should also remind us that it is individuals that make history, not some indiscriminate blending of impersonal forces that succeed in swallowing up individual agency. In short, it is important to note that there was nothing inevitable about Reagan's success. Today, with the benefit of hindsight, numerous accounts of the conservative movement have a kind of "triumphalist" inevitability about them. But as even a cursory review of the movement can attest, the success of conservatism was anything but inevitable. It depended on particular victories at particular times, based on particular decisions by particular individuals, most notably by Ronald Reagan himself.

Reagan's career, and especially the fall of the Soviet Union, is one of those times in history where, if one is a believer, one can talk about the hand of providence, and if one is not, one can talk about coincidence and good fortune. Either way, it is remarkable what happened then. If one had said in 1975 that Margaret Thatcher, an obscure British junior cabinet minister, would challenge Edward Heath, her party's leader, and then become the first woman ever to lead the Conservative Party in Britain, later defeating Labor's Jim Callaghan to become the first female prime minister in British history, and holding that position for eleven years, few would have believed that wildly improbable prediction. Similarly, who would have thought that in 1978 Pope John Paul I would die within a month of his election, and then be succeeded by a Polish cardinal who would serve for over twenty-five years and be arguably the most influential pope in modern history? Finally, who would have believed that Ronald Reagan, after serving two terms as governor of California and losing a primary challenge to an incumbent president, would, at age sixty-nine, become the oldest person ever elected president of the United States?

Nevertheless, this was indeed the set of circumstances that transpired, so that by January 1981, Reagan, Thatcher, and Pope John Paul II all held crucial positions in the Western world at a moment of great opportunity and great vulnerability. Within ten years, the Soviet Union was gone. It is safe to say that very few people had any sense that the Soviet Union was so vulnerable, but this vulnerability would probably have not been so thoroughly exposed without the combination of Thatcher's resolve, Reagan's defense buildup and assistance to resistance fighters around the world, and Pope John Paul II's historic visit to Poland in June 1979, which helped give rise to the Solidarity movement. That all of these things happened at once, and that within ten years the Soviet Empire was peacefully dissolved, is really an amazing historical fact.

In retrospect, we should appreciate the importance of those individuals. It is a reminder that history does not move simply because of massive social forces or even massive movements of ideas or cultural forces, but is moved by individuals and their ability to acquire authority and then exercise it in bold and daring ways.

Reagan's Legacy

At the end of the Reagan administration, the universal view among conservatives was that the movement had helped the economy rebound by implementing tax cuts, exercising fiscal restraint with regard to domestic spending, taming inflation, and reducing interest rates—an impressive feat given the depths of economic stagflation during the Carter administration. And of course, there were several successful foreign policy initiatives, most particularly the great victory against Soviet communism.

However, on the broader cultural, social, and moral front, despite Reagan's personal views and impressive rhetoric, less progress was made. In fact, the 1980s were a disappointing decade in terms of a number of social and cultural indicators that are too numerous to list here, but that are quite familiar to movement conservatives. In particular, the attempt to restore the courts to their proper role, to restore constitutionalism, to delimit judicial power in an appropriate way, were stymied by the defeat of Robert Bork's Supreme Court nomination in 1987. That defeat was devastating for the conservative movement, especially when combined with the appointment of Sandra Day O'Connor to the Supreme Court, a rare lapse of judgment for Reagan. Overall, conservatives were quite right to be pessimistic about the moral and cultural status of American society, especially given the moral backsliding that occurred during the Clinton years.

Nevertheless, the trend in this arena is now subtly turning, and with the confirmation of John Roberts and Samuel Alito to the high court, it would appear that these positive social and cultural trends will finally find an ally in this newly reconstituted Court. Although Reagan lost the Bork nomination, both Roberts and Alito are jurists who came to Washington during the Reagan administration, when the federal courts were being populated with prudent advocates of judicial restraint. So, in a way, Reagan has finally won, posthumously, his battle to reshape the Court in an originalist fashion. Of course, this fight is by no means over, as the Court is pretty ideologically balanced. Most agree, for instance, that it would take two or three more solid appointments for strict constructionists to dominate the court, but there is no doubt that Reagan's judicial appointments were crucial to this overall effort.

And as we look to the future of conservatism, it is safe to say that these issues of judicial politics will once again assume center stage on the political agenda, so much so that a huge fight over the next appointment to the Court could dwarf all other issues, save the Iraq War. I do not know if conservatives and Republicans in the Bush administration are fully ready for this fight, but folks at the grassroots certainly are, and there will certainly be a role for them to play in this ongoing political drama. If President Bush does not have another appointment, the next presidential election will be run with a Court that is evenly divided, one that is clearly going to have one, two, or three vacancies in the next presidential term. This issue, of all Reagan's issues, will undoubtedly dominate future American politics—over twenty years after his leaving office.

Finally, we will have two of the most wide-open races for the 2008 presidential nominations ever, which will certainly mean a larger market for fresh ideas and a clear debate over the future direction of both major political parties. This promises to be a very healthy thing for the Republican Party and for the conservative movement, especially after the internecine conflict of the Bush II era. The politicians will definitely not like it; they never like turmoil, disarray, and debate. But if we can learn anything from the legacy of Ronald Reagan, it is that open debate, courage, and challenging conventional wisdom can actually be a very healthy thing.

Notes

Introduction

1. George H. Nash, *The Conservative Intellectual Movement in America Since 1945* (New York: Basic Books, 1976): xi.
2. For a fuller discussion of these points, see: Charles W. Dunn, "Conservatism," in *Encyclopedia of Politics and Religion*, 2nd ed. (Washington, DC: CQ Press, 2007); Charles W. Dunn, *The Seven Laws of Presidential Leadership* (Upper Saddle River, NJ: Pearson/Prentice-Hall, 2007); Charles W. Dunn and J. David Woodard, *The Conservative Tradition in America* (Lanham, MD: Rowman & Littlefield, 2003); Charles W. Dunn, ed., *Faith, Freedom, and the Future: Religion in American Political Culture* (Lanham, MD: Rowman & Littlefield, 2003); Charles W. Dunn, *The Scarlet Thread of Scandal: Morality and the American Presidency* (Lanham, MD: Rowman & Littlefield, 2000); and Charles W. Dunn, *American Political Theology* (New York: Praeger, 1984).
3. Abraham Lincoln, Address, Cooper Union, New York, February 27, 1860.
4. Lionel Trilling, *The Liberal Imagination* (New York: Viking, 1960): ix.
5. Frederick von Hayek, *The Road to Serfdom*, 17th ed. (Chicago: University of Chicago Press, 1956).
6. Richard Weaver, *Ideas Have Consequences* (Chicago: University of Chicago Press, 1948).
7. Ludwig von Mises, *Human Action* (Chicago: Regnery, 1966)
8. Peter Viereck, *Conservatism Revisited* (New York: Greenwood Press, 1978).
9. William F. Buckley Jr., *God and Man at Yale*, 2nd ed. (Chicago: Regnery, 1977).
10. Eric Voegelin, *The New Science of Politics* (Chicago: University of Chicago Press, 1952).
11. Russell Kirk, *The Conservative Mind: From Burke to Eliot*, 7th ed. (Chicago: Regnery, 1986).
12. Leo Strauss, *Natural Right and History* (Chicago: University of Chicago Press, 1953).
13. Robert Nisbet, *The Quest for Community* (New York: Oxford University Press, 1953).
14. Clinton Rossiter, *Conservatism in America* (New York: Knopf, 1955).
15. Milton Friedman, *Capitalism and Freedom* (Chicago: University of Chicago Press, 1962).

16. James M. Buchanan and Richard E. Wagner, *The Calculus of Consent: Logical Foundations of Constitutional Democracy* (Ann Arbor, MI: University of Michigan Press, 1962).

17. Forrest McDonald, *E Pluribus Unum* (Lawrence, KS: University Press of Kansas, 1965).

18. Edward Banfield, *The Unheavenly City* (Boston: Little, Brown, 1970).

19. Harvey C. Mansfield, *The Spirit of Liberalism* (Cambridge, MA: Harvard University Press, 1978).

20. George Gilder, *Wealth and Poverty* (New York: Basic Books, 1981).

21. Herbert Storing, *What the Anti-Federalists Were For: The Political Thought of the Opponents of the Constitution* (Chicago: University of Chicago Press, 1981).

22. Richard John Neuhaus, *The Naked Public Square* (Grand Rapids, MI: Eerdmans, 1984).

23. Charles Murray, *Losing Ground* (New York: Basic Books, 1984).

24. Allan Bloom, *The Closing of the American Mind* (New York: Simon & Schuster, 1987).

25. E. D. Hirsch Jr., *Cultural Literacy* (Boston: Houghton Mifflin, 1987).

26. Shelby Steele, *The Content of Our Character: A New Vision of Race in America* (New York: St. Martin's, 1991).

27. Arnold Toynbee, *A Study of History* (London: Oxford University Press, 1948).

28. For an analysis of language in democracy, see: Joshua M. Dunn, "Tocqueville, Nietzsche, and the Family Values Debate," University of Virginia, Unpublished Paper, December 16, 1997; and for an analysis of conservatism, modernism, and postmodernism, see: Jennifer Mahurin, "The Power of Rhetorical Conservatism," Grove City College, Unpublished Paper, April 22, 2002.

29. Weaver, *Ideas Have Consequences*.

Chapter 3

1. See, for example, John Micklethwait and Adrian Wooldridge, "Cheer Up Conservatives, You're Still Winning," *Wall Street Journal*, Tuesday, 21 June 2005, A16. The authors of this piece are also the authors of *The Right Nation: Conservative Power in America* (New York: Penguin Press, 2004) which traces the rise of conservatism through its various organizations and programs from the 1950s into the first term of George W. Bush.

2. This fact, to my knowledge, has not been widely reported in the mainstream media. That there is a gulf within conservative ranks can be seen in the columns of certain syndicated columnists—e.g., Patrick Buchanan, Paul Craig Roberts—long regarded as conservatives. Certainly the pages of *Chronicles* and the *American Conservative* reflect what would appear to be an unbridgeable divide. Likewise a division among intellectual conservatives is evident in the Philadelphia Society.

3. I base this upon conversations and correspondence with numerous traditional conservatives of long acquaintance.

4. Even on these issues, some questions have been raised by social conservatives regarding the commitment of the Bush II administration. See, for instance, W. James Antle, "Republican Stepchildren," *American Conservative*, 11 April 2005.

5. Robert Nisbet's *The Present Age* (New York: Harper & Row, 1988), for example, is a devastating critique of the acknowledged principles that guide Bush II's foreign policy.

6. The fact that she prematurely fixes the birth of the Bill of Rights is of no matter. What

142

is of greater concern is what purpose, if any, she had in mind by lumping the Bill of Rights and the Constitution together.

7. Http://www.state.gov/secretary/rm/2005/ 41973.htm.

8. This linkage may have been intended. Some traditionalists contend that the goals of Bush II's foreign policy and the Iraq War are a modern extension of the underlying principles and tenets of the French Revolution. See Claes Ryn, *America the Virtuous: The Crisis of Democracy and the Quest for Empire* (Somerset, NJ: Transaction Publishers, 2003).

9. This transformation, of course, causes problems for organizations such as the American Conservative Union, which finds it increasingly difficult to support both the president and its principles. Pragmatic considerations almost invariably lead such organizations to scrap principle and support party, otherwise they would probably not survive. My impression is that in acknowledged conservative circles the more politically active tend to sublimate principle to party. It is also my impression that most Americans, for a number of reasons, do not experience any cognitive dissonance between party and principle. If and when they do, party seems to trump principle most of the time.

10. James Burnham, *Congress and the American Tradition* (Chicago: H. Regnery Co., 1959).

11. Woodrow Wilson, *Constitutional Government in the United States* (New York, 1908; reprint, 1961), 81.

12. See, for example, James MacGregor Burns, *Deadlock of Democracy* (Englewood Cliffs, NJ: Prentice Hall, 1963). His final chapter, "Strategy for Americans," synthesizes many of the elements of party reform that have been advanced over the decades and emphasizes the need for parties to "build grass-roots memberships" that are united with the leadership through "their common faith in their party's tradition, doctrine, and policy."

13. We may speculate that this new dimension of presidential power—i.e., that which stems from the wide latitude he enjoys as both leader and privileged "prince" of his political party—can ultimately be traced to the decline of political parties at the local levels, a decline brought about, in part, by efforts to democratize the parties.

14. Wilson, *Constitutional Government in the United States*, 68.

15. Clinton Rossiter writes that "there have been moments of triumph or dedication or frustration or even shame when the will of the people—the General Will, I suppose we could call it—demanded to be heard clearly and unmistakably." Since the time of Jackson, he continues, presidents have assumed the "prerogative" to do so; "to act, . . . in Wilson's words, as "'the spokesman for the real sentiment and purpose of the country.'" *The American Presidency* (New York: Harcourt Brace, 1956), 18.

16. It is a maxim of American politics that a president never wants to preside over the diminishment of presidential powers and prerogatives. He never wants to leave the office weaker, constitutionally or otherwise, than when he entered it. This would be the sign of a "weak" or failed presidency.

17. A similar explanation can be offered for the behavior of judges, particularly those on the Supreme Court. There is a widespread suspicion often articulated that judges who move "left" do so to acquire respectability in the quarters that "count." In the eyes of the *New York Times* editorial board, Justice Anthony Kennedy, upon abandoning a conservative outlook on key issues, was said to have "grown" in office.

18. I am referring here to his analysis on the ways in which power can be thwarted and controlled when necessary as presented in *On Power* (Indianapolis: HarperBusiness, 1994).

19. Experience has shown that the War Powers Resolution of 1973 intended to ameliorate this problem, has been far from effective. Presidents, both Republican and Democratic, have largely ignored it. The reasons for their defiance are largely those I note in the text; presidents look upon this act as an encroachment on their institutional powers.

20. In this regard, one thinks of the Iran-Contra investigation during the Reagan era, the debate in the Senate over Bush I's Gulf War policy, and Clinton's initial reluctance to commit forces to the Balkans. More telling, in light of what I say below, is that the Vietnam War did not arouse effective congressional scrutiny under Johnson's administration. Rather, this scrutiny began in earnest under Nixon with a divided government.

21. Thus, I would modify Willmoore Kendall's analysis and conclusion set forth in "Two Majorities," *Midwest Journal of Political Science* 4 (November, 1960). The Congress is inherently more conservative than the presidency, but only when an institutional independence in the sense I have indicated above will allow it to reveal its true character.

Chapter 4

1. Samuel Huntington, *Who are We? The Challenges to American National Identity* (New York: Simon and Schuster, 2004).
2. The phrase is from Adam Smith's *The Wealth of Nations*.
3. Samuel Sherwood, "The Church's Flight Into the Wilderness" (1776), in Ellis Sandoz, ed., *Political Sermons of the American Founding Era 1730–1805* (Indianapolis: Liberty Fund, 1990), 503.

Chapter 5

1. Alexis de Tocqueville, *Democracy in America*, Harvey C. Mansfield and Delba Winthrop eds. (Chicago: University of Chicago Press, 2000) II 4.3, 6, 644, 663.
2. Aristotle, *Rhetoric* II 13.
3. "In framing a government which is to be administered by men over men, the great difficulty lies in this: you must first enable the government to control the governed, and in the next place oblige it to control itself." *Federalist* 51.
4. See David Epstein, *The Political Theory of the Federalist* (Chicago: University of Chicago Press, 1984), 179–84; Harvey C. Mansfield Jr., *Taming the Prince* (Baltimore, MD: Johns Hopkins University Press, 1993), 270–71, 291–93.
5. The classic work is Harry V. Jaffa's *Crisis of the House Divided*, to which one may add more recent books by Allen C. Guelzo and Richard Striner.

Chapter 6

1. See Aurel Kolnai, "The Meaning of the 'Common Man'," in Kolnai, *Privilege and Liberty*, ed. by Daniel J. Mahoney (Lanham, MD: Lexington Books, 1999), 64.
2. Charles Kesler, "Democracy and the Bush Doctrine," *Claremont Review of Books* 5, no. 1 (Winter 2004), 18.
3. This point was central to Charles de Gaulle's famous "Bayeux address" of June 16, 1946.
4. Alexis de Tocqueville, *The Old Regime and the Regime*, trans. by Alan S. Kahan (Chicago: University of Chicago Press, 1998), 3, 3, 217.

5. Kesler, "Democracy and the Bush Doctrine," 20.
6. Pierre Manent, *A World beyond Politics?: A Defense of the Nation-State*, trans. by Marc LePain (Princeton, NJ: Princeton University Press, 2006), viii.
7. Ibid.

Chapter 7

1. See my book *Fighting for Liberty and Virtue: Political and Cultural Wars in Eighteenth Century America* (Wheaton, IL: Crossway Books and Regnery, 1995).
2. The Heritage Foundation in numerous reports has documented well the statistical difference that religious involvement makes, and I have examined this journalistically in *Compassionate Conservatism* (2000).
3. Rather than running from debates about abortion we should take on those like Princeton Professor Peter Singer who say that unborn children can be killed because they lack higher mental capacities. We need to add a bit of vision to the debate. Why not destroy acorns, because they are utterly lacking in material for chairs or houses? Several years ago, when I rose to the utmost level of my coaching abilities by becoming a Pony League assistant coach, I spent time with kids who didn't throw or catch all that well. The Singer doctrine would indicate that I was wasting my time, since they lacked higher baseball capacities. Of course, so did I.

Index

Index

Index

Index

natural law, 28, 44
natural right: faith and, 28; the French
Revolution and, 45; neoconservatism and,
23–24
natural selection, 126
nature, 49
Nazism, 46
neoconservatism: American foreign policy
and, 68; anti-totalitarian position of, 66–67;
George W. Bush and, 15–16; characterized,
vi–vii; emergence of, 7–8; foundational
concept, 23–24; Francis Fukuyama and, 67–
68; Irving Kristol's definition of, 7; objections
to liberalism, 26; partnership in leadership
with the Religious Right, 28–29; present-day
indictments of, 67–69; rhetoric of democracy
and, 72–74; traditional conservatism and,
12–13, 32. *See also* second neoconservatism
new conservatism, 4
New Deal, 104–5
New Left, 7
Niemeyer, Gerhart, 4
Nietzsche, Friedrich, 47
nihilism, 118–19
Nisbet, Robert, vii, 4
Nixon, Richard M., 108, 110, 135

O

O'Connor, Sandra Day, 138
Office for Population Affairs, 109
Old Testament: the Holy Land in, 80–81;
Israelites' behavior in the Holy Land, 83–84; on
living outside ancient Israel, 87–88
one-income families, 110, 111
order, 24
ordered freedom, 6
orthodox Christians, 114
O'Sullivan, John, 13–14
OutFest, 86
ownership, iv, 44

P

paleoconservatism: characterized, vii; criticism
of neoconservatives, 12–13; perceptions of
the Bush administration, 32. *See also* traditional conservatism
parenthood, 120
partial-birth abortion, 109
Pascal, Blaise, 129
Passion of Christ, The (film), 82
Paul, Saint, 83, 89, 91, 92
personal responsibility, iii–iv
Philadelphia Inquirer, 87
Planned Parenthood, 103
Podhoretz, Norman, vi, 7
political coalitions, 81
Political Economy Research Center (PERC), 10
political parties: one-party control of
government and, 39–41; overcoming the
separation of powers and, 38; power-sharing
and, 41; the presidency and, 34, 35–36;
presidents' transformation of, 32–33, 34, 38,
41; role of, 35
politics: intellectualization of, 11
popular culture, 62–63
populism, 53, 54
populist conservatism, 12
"pork barrel" projects, 34
Possony, Stefan, 4
postmodern democracy, 76–77
postmodernism, ix, 46
presidency: Congress and, 34–35; growth in
power of, 35; need for counterweight to, 41;
political parties and, 34, 35–36; separation
from popular will and, 53–54
presidential elections: Reagan and, 7, 108–9,
135, 136; recent electoral trends in, 58, 59,
60, 61; virtue voters in 2004, 130–31
presidential leadership, 35–36
presidents: desire for a "legacy," 40–41;
incumbents, 37–38; one-party control of
government and, 39–41; pathological egoism

153

Index

About the Editor

Charles W. Dunn, dean of Regent University's Robertson School of Government, has authored or edited fifteen books, including *The Seven Laws of Presidential Leadership*; *The Conservative Tradition in America*; *Faith, Freedom, and the Future: Religion in American Political Culture*; and *The Scarlet Thread of Scandal: Morality and the American Presidency*. He has taught at Florida State University, the University of Illinois, Clemson University, and Grove City College. President Ronald Reagan appointed him to the J. William Fulbright Foreign Scholarship Board, which he chaired for four terms.